About the Author

I am a very fortunate man to have two healthy and confident children, and an incredible partner who holds my hand through the maze of life and parenting, my wife Laura. I have been blessed with two incredibly loving and supportive parents, the bar is set very high, and I intend to be the best possible parent I can be. I am very grateful to have had this book published and sincerely hope it encourages more conversations about the unmet needs of contemporary parenting in the UK.

Breaking Dad:
Man-Up Snowflake

Baz Price

Breaking Dad:
Man-Up Snowflake

Olympia Publishers
London

www.olympiapublishers.com
OLYMPIA PAPERBACK EDITION

Copyright © Baz Price 2023

The right of Baz Price to be identified as author of
this work has been asserted in accordance with sections 77 and 78
of the Copyright, Designs and Patents Act 1988.

All Rights Reserved

No reproduction, copy or transmission of this publication
may be made without written permission.
No paragraph of this publication may be reproduced,
copied or transmitted save with the written permission of the
publisher, or in accordance with the provisions
of the Copyright Act 1956 (as amended).

Any person who commits any unauthorised act in relation to
this publication may be liable to criminal
prosecution and civil claims for damage.

A CIP catalogue record for this title is
available from the British Library.

ISBN: 978-1-80074-547-6

First Published in 2023

The opinions expressed in this book are the author's own and do
not reflect the views of the publisher, author's employer,
organisation, committee or other group or individual.

Olympia Publishers
Tallis House
2 Tallis Street
London
EC4Y 0AB

Printed in Great Britain

Dedication

This is for you, Dad. I miss you every day, and I will always aspire to live up to your legacy.

Acknowledgements

Thank you to my wife, Laura, for never dampening my randomness, for being my inspiration and for the ongoing adventure of raising our two beautiful little humans together.

Contents

Prologue 13
RELEVANT DEFINITIONS (According to the Collins
English Dictionary) 17
1 Agenda 23
2 Protected Characteristics 43
3 So what is this Shared Parental Leave policy all about? ... 70
4 Equality Landmarks 78
4 Unconscious Bias 89
5 Our Story 98
7 It's OK, we have an Equality and Diversity policy 101
8 The Hunt for Support: Take 1 116
9 Societal Benefits of Parental Equality 120
10 Hunt for support: Take 2 Time to become a 'Union Man'
.... 138
11 Delay, Deny, Defend 140
12 Hunt for Support: Take 3 The Citizens' Advice Bureau
.... 151
13 Hunt for Support: Take 4 Charity Begins at Home
(Insurance) 155
14 Going for Gold 157
15. The Great 'Bundle' Bungle 167
16 My day in court! (Rabbit in the proverbial headlights) . 177
17 Noggin above the parapet 197

18 Define 'Disrepute' 202
19 The Authority Flex 207
20 Strategy or Calamity? 222
21 Cap in Hand 235
22 All aboard the Appeal Train! 241
23 Employment Appeal Tribunal Hearing Day-ja vu The Last Crusade! 245
24 Judge Judy and Executioner 248
25 The Verdict 252
26 Conclusion 255
Aftermath – Lessons Learned 255

Prologue

The following is my personal account, as a new biological father, concerning the archaic and stereotypical 'Black Hole' that is the parental rights of the father in mid Wales in 2018-19. Overall, sadly it is a true account of the vast majority of employers in the rest of the United Kingdom too.

My account is a hybrid of a cautionary tale regarding taking on a local authority solo, and a reminder that if we do not step up and speak up when we experience social injustice, we are accountable for its continuance.

Shared Parental Leave is the exception to the rule of equality and diversity. Why? Because of an age-old patriarchal society where men have been the enemy. You cannot say 'Boogieman' without the word 'man.'

In February 2018, I, a male employee in my tenth year in post, emailed Human Resources on behalf of myself and my wife (three months pregnant at the time) to throw out an inquiry email regarding the available provisions available at The Authority. After discussing with my line manager in supervision in April 2018 that my wife would like to return to her job two weeks after birth (if all was well) and I wanted to take the Lion's share, I sent a structured follow-up email to HR requesting a breakdown of my entitlements. In hindsight our optimism in buying into The Authority's 'Equality and Diversity policy' and 'Council Values' (championing progressiveness, equality, diversity, and zero tolerance on discrimination) was very, very naive. The word tokenism springs to mind with regard to the marginalised and forgotten rights of the biological father. Since April 2018, we have embarked upon an absolutely bonkers and farcical journey littered by shoddiness caused directly by The Authority and the departments therein. To date this has resulted in us losing our case 'unanimously' at an Employment Tribunal Hearing in September 2019.

We have subsequently felt The Authority's wrath after I exercised my civil right to petition for them not providing enhanced pay for biological fathers, when they do so for biological mums on Maternity Leave and the elected adoptive parent within the Adoption Leave policy. The advice to me from a senior manager was 'You have made your point, now wind your neck in.'

I struggled to decide upon just one quote to sum up my family's experience over this whacky ole journey. Therefore, I have compromised with the following three:

THE GREATEST ENEMY OF CLEAR LANGUAGE IS INSINCERITY.
GEORGE ORWELL.

IN THE MIDST OF CHAOS, THERE IS ALSO OPPORTUNITY.
SUN TZU. THE ART OF WAR.

SHAKIN' STEVENS. 'THIS OLE HOUSE.'

Taking on 'The Man' is a lonely old stress-riddled pastime. Not to mention a stereotypically sexist one too. I prefer to say that we have taken on the establishment, given the irony of the 'all-powerful' gender assumption of 'The Man.' It won't be until this message is shared amongst common thinkers that it will hopefully gather momentum and become the catalyst for meaningful conversations. Hopefully, in time, our momentum will merge with other likeminded people who have also popped their heads above the parapet, and then, my friends, you have a movement. Then and only then will the narrative have a chance of adapting to meet our contemporary requirements in achieving social justice. By changing the overall landscape for the better of everyone in society as the law and policy makers will have to appreciate the sheer gravity of the much needed reform.

Expectations of fathers have never been as high. I get it, that guys like me chuntering on about parental equal rights adds to these expectations. That is not my aim. My aim is to unlock and swing open wide the door of choice for fathers. To be more hands on if they want to and if it suits the dynamic of their family and their parental partnership.

This whole book is my journal, as a new dad, on how to (and more importantly, how not to) challenge societal wrongs. I am going to take you down the rabbit hole of the baffling oddities of bygone ways and the bonkers ineptitude of 'The Man'.

Dignity always prevails (eventually).

RELEVANT DEFINITIONS
(According to the Collins English Dictionary)

Equality
Equality is the same status, rights, and responsibilities for all the members of a society, group, or family.

Diversity
The diversity of something is the fact that it contains many very different elements.

Progressiveness
Someone who is progressive or has progressive ideas has modern ideas about how things should be done, rather than traditional ones.

Principles
A set of standards or rules of personal conduct.

Values
The moral principles and beliefs or accepted standards of a person or social group.

Tokenism
If you refer to an action as tokenism, you disapprove of it because you think it is just done for effect, in order to show a particular intention or to impress a particular type of person.

Social Justice
The principle that all members of a society have equal rights and opportunities.

Civil Rights
The rights that people have in a society to equal treatment and equal opportunities, whatever their race, sex, or religion.

Free Speech
Free speech is the right to express your opinions in public.

Bureaucracy
A bureaucracy is an administrative system operated by a large number of officials.

Red Tape
You refer to official rules and procedures as red tape when they seem unnecessary and cause delays.

Gender Bias
Prejudice based on gender.

Marginalize
To marginalize a group of people means to make them feel isolated and unimportant.

Overlook
If you overlook a fact or problem, you do not notice it, or do not realize how important it is.

Scapegoat
If you say that someone is made a scapegoat for something bad that has happened, you mean that people blame them and may punish them for it although it may not be their fault.

Disrepute
If something is brought into disrepute or falls into disrepute, it loses its good reputation, because it is connected with activities that people do not approve of.

Spin
If someone puts a certain spin on an event or situation, they interpret it and try to present it in a particular way.

RELEVANT DEFINITIONS (According to what I have learned along the way, aka mansplaining)

Clusterf*ckery
When it appears nigh on impossible to see any common sense and a trail of clown-like debris is scattered all over the shop.

Fubar
F*cked Up Beyond All Recognition! When all around you have lost their capability to be of any use whatsoever. Utter despondency in the inability of the useless.

Being driven 'Incre-mental'

The long-drawn-out swamp of reluctance to move towards even the acknowledgement of the social injustice. The whole grinding and unnecessary unsupportive process took me from being a confident and happy guy, into an all-round exhausted, frazzled, and anxious guy. I became an old frayed rope in much need of repair. How is it used in a sentence? The thousands of hours I have put into this grievance, where I have butted heads with institutionalised and bureaucratic resistance gradually affected my mental and physical health in an incre-mental way.

Testicle Tax

I coined this phrase in order to accurately highlight how biological fathers (who mostly have testicles) are penalised financially (taxed) when accessing the 2015 Shared Parental Leave within the UK. Evidenced by the basic minimum statutory pay available for biological dads, in comparison to the enhanced pay provided for adoptive parents and birth mums.

Motherhood Penalty

The detrimental effect on a mother's career progression as a result of society's generalised expectation that the mum should take a career break in order to take the sole responsibility for the nurture and care of their baby.

Man up

(Urban Dictionary definition)
To build up enough courage (usually for men) to face adversity and responsibility.

Snowflake
(Urban Dictionary definition)

A term for someone who thinks they are unique and special, but really are not. It gained popularity after the movie *Fight Club* from the quote 'You are not special. You're not a beautiful and unique snowflake. You're the same decaying matter as everything else.'

Began being used extensively as a putdown for someone, usually on the political left, who is easily offended or felt they needed a 'safe space' away from the harsh realities of the world, but now has morphed into a general putdown for anyone that complains about any subject.

Misandry
A hatred of men.

Examples of misandry in a Sentence. Recent Examples on the Web. '"Matriarchy Now" was encouraging misandry and oppressing men.' — Sebastian Matthew, Billboard, 'Meet The 17-Year-Old Activist Behind New Line "Matriarchy Now"', 24th August, 2017.

(Merriam-Webster)

1
Agenda

'He who is not courageous enough to take risks in life will accomplish nothing in life.' Muhammad Ali.

My name is Baz Price. At the time of writing, I am a thirty-six-year-old, first-time father of a thirteen-month-old beautiful, confident, and healthy daughter. My partner in our parental rollercoaster is my wife of just over two years, Laura, aka Mummy.

Let us start this story way back when. Back in May 1982, my dad Geoff and my mum Jan got it on. They had a hankering for a second child. Their first son Gav, my only brother, was three years old. Out of the thirty-nine million sperms vying for the ultimate prize of making it to the egg, my trooper made it. Me. This lucky bastard who's typing these words. In addition to overcoming these incredible odds, my folks went for my first scan in Brecon War Memorial hospital in August 1982. It was here that the sonographer informed them that I had spina bifida. This is a birth defect where there is an incompletion of closing of the spinal cord, which affects the ability to walk and control the bladder and bowel. In a nutshell, it has life changing complications for baby and parents. Mum was referred to a specialist centre in Newport, South Wales. It was there that mum was asked, 'Where would you like to go for your abortion?' Mum and Dad both refused the medical assumption and continued with the pregnancy. If it was not for their call, I would have not had the absolute pleasure of winning Erwood Village Show's 'Most Beautiful Baby' competition in 1983. What a travesty that would have been for the marvel and pageantry of such an elite sport.

In January 1983, I was born at Brecon War Memorial Hospital in mid Wales without Spina Bifida or any other physical issues. The first baby to be born on said premises via a birthing stool. It was literally a stool with a hole in the seat. As true as I am typing this, I entered the world with such speed (and grace) that I slipped through the awaiting poised hands of the midwife and landed on the maternity ward floor. Thankfully, I took it like a champ and suffered no ill effects. I can see the scene in my mind's eye now. Like an abseiling accident due to some overzealous belaying.

The miracle that is the conception of life and dodging two other bullets before I made my first squawk, means that I have to prove my worthiness of such insurmountable fortune. It seems appropriate that the campaign I find myself in, thirty-five years later, is very apt given the unconditional love and faith invested in my own birth by my loving parents.

Our agenda has (and will always be) about clarity, openness, and opportunity to overcome unconscious biases against the rights of the biological father and the parental role in general. Our aim has never been (and never will be) to embarrass or damage my employer's reputation. I have a civil and human right to make a grievance and to petition against discrimination. I have based our challenge on fact, experience, and the literal policies of my employer. Namely their 'Council Values' and 'Equality and Diversity Policy.'

We want to live in a society where parents have the right to choose how they manage their own parental leave in a manner which best suits the family's needs. Paid paternity leave has been in place in Sweden since 1974 and in Iceland since 2000. The idea being that it offers fathers more freedom to look after their baby, and to strengthen the mother's position within the labour market. It does not take a rocket scientist to recognise how advantageous this concept is for closing the Gender Pay Gap and the Gender Care Gap.

We (the United Kingdom) rock up in 2015 with a p*ss poor afterthought, and label a policy 'Shared Parental Leave'. Which sounds like an all-encompassing celebration of equality. By only offering the basic statutory minimum pay to do so, it is less of a celebration and more of a damning reflection of how sexist the UK is when it comes to parental rights. When you consider that working women in the UK have been benefitting from Maternity Leave (with enhanced pay) since the 1975 Employment Protection Act (a year later than Sweden introduced the gender-neutral, paid parental leave) forty-four years later fathers are still not treated equally with regards to parental rights on the whole in the UK. The disparity is beyond embarrassing in a so-called modern and progressive society such as ours. The unconscious bias needs a complete overhaul if it is ever going to achieve equality and dissolve parental stereotypes.

The purpose of sharing our family's experience over the first few years of our daughter's life comes in the aftermath of us losing our Sex Discrimination case at an Employment Tribunal Hearing against my employer, 'The Authority.' I think it's very important to note straight off the bat that we are not bad losers, hell-bent on getting our pound of flesh from

The Authority. Our gripe is a wider gripe against all employers within the UK and beyond who are yet to embrace equality for all parents. Especially the forgotten biological parent. The Dad.

It is important to highlight that there are a number of trailblazers such as Goldman Sachs, Vodafone, Aviva, the National Health Service, and the Welsh Government, who have recognised the discrimination present within the Shared Parental Leave policy and have taken it upon themselves to offer enhanced pay, on par with Maternity Leave policy provisions, to provide a level playing field for parents.

Regardless of gender or type of parent (e.g. biological, adoptive, male, female, and any other denomination that a parent might identify as), I am by no means gunning for my employers in an attempt to tarnish their public image or shine any individuals in an unsavoury light. What I am trying to achieve is to highlight the absence of equality for biological fathers whose only route to parental leave at my place of work is via the Shared Parental Leave policy. A sham of a policy which only offers the basic statutory minimum pay (nothing additional) rendering it only accessible for wealthier parents who can 'take the hit' financially. 'Don't be a snowflake, that's a nationwide policy,' I hear you say. This is true for the majority of employers in 2019. However, at my place of work, my employers offer biological mothers enhanced pay over and above the statutory minimum payment because of the physical and psychological impact of pregnancy, childbirth, recovery, and maternal bonding. That is the law. Sounds absolutely correct, that mum's are entitled to the enhanced pay. Most likeminded people would agree with me.

'So, what's your problem snowflake?' I hear you ask. I

use the term 'snowflake' with a touch of frivolity as an individual, who shall remain nameless, took great exception to my claim of social injustice in one of our local newspapers' online articles, The County Times. The 'Keyboard Warrior' referred to me as a 'Snowflake' and added that I needed to stop being so soft and get on with it! Bless their progressive socks. I was sat in my car in a high school car park post appointment with a pupil when I read said opinion. It was a forty-minute drive and I spent the majority of that time thinking of witty comebacks to shame their ignorance and pointing out how her view is a barrier to achieving equality. I concluded that the benefits of any keyboard warrior to and froing would have distracted from the point I was trying to make. I was already knackered from juggling being a partner with my wife, a first-time dad, an extended family member, a friend, and an employee. The last thing I needed to do was get into a Monty Python type argument of who is worse off with a random, 'man-up' and defend 'Team Snowflake.' There is no rationalising with the irrational. I could see it now, a reminder of how precious I am being and how great I have it, from a person I have never met. 'You were lucky. We lived for three months in a brown paper bag in a septic tank. We used to have to get up at six o'clock in the morning, clean the bag, eat a crust of stale bread, go to work down mill for fourteen hours a day week-in-week-out. When we got home, our dad would thrash us to sleep with his belt.' Monty Python – The 4 Yorkshiremen.

 Our problem is that adoptive parents at my place of work (and rightly so I will pre-empt) also receive the enhanced pay and provisions in accordance with the Maternity Leave policy. Hmm, where is the justification for this? Given that the adoptive parent does not experience the aforementioned consequences of pregnancy and childbirth, why are their rights valued in higher esteem than biological fathers at my place of work, who are not entitled to these provisions? Another factor which is a given (rightly so) with adoption is the ongoing support from an Adoption Team Social Worker throughout the adopted child's formative years. Again, I want to be clear, this support is an imperative framework that is appropriate and necessary. As a biological parent, I am not supported throughout my daughter's formative years by a professional social worker and respective adoption social work team. At the end of the day, a parent is a parent regardless of their gender or label. If we are responsible for a little human, we are a parent and should be treated equally, full stop. There is the unambiguous bottom line. The clear water before it gets muddied by bureaucracy, policies, silo cultures, legal comparators, and gender bias stereotypes.

The pressures as a biological father have been evidenced in several published psychological studies, such as 'Promoting Postpartum Mental Health in Fathers: Recommendations for Nurse Practitioners'. This study from the American Journal 2018 shines an unprecedented light on how detrimental the parental pressures are for biological fathers too. There is evidence that there is an increase in depression with dads. In an age where society is moving towards the promotion of talking about our own mental health, it blows me away how the rights of fathers are still being forgotten, thus reinforcing the stereotype that only the mother can nurture the baby. The dad's physiological and psychological makeup is stressed upon throughout pregnancy, child birth, and the subsequent parental support where we are expected to hit the ground running in an attempt to achieve excellence in providing for, guiding, and protecting a brand new human being. Oh and at the same time being there as an equal partner in the life we share with the mum and all the external responsibilities of parenting. Such as, being shoehorned by society to conform to the breadwinning stereotype and get back down that mine after two weeks paternity leave, while the little wife stays at home to raise the baby. What year are we in again?

The first of many examples to prove the 'forgotten tag' for dads is the lack of recognition from the very esteemed legal powers that be (Court of Appeal, 2019), who emphasised that birth mums deserved the enhanced pay during their maternity leave and dads should not on their Shared Parental Leave. One of their arguments for this is the need for a baby to be nurtured and bond with the mother. There is an ignored fundamental importance of recognising that dads need to bond with their baby as much as the birth mum. I wholeheartedly disagree with the Court of Appeal's decision. Not only is it the mother's right and the father's right to bond with their baby, more importantly it is the child's right to have equal care and nurture from both parents. Attachment Disorder is widely acknowledged within children's services in Wales (surely across the rest of the UK too) as being a marker of early childhood trauma which can have a detrimental impact on development, interpersonal skills and can hinder empathy development.

By far the most shaming piece of legislature is present within The United Nations Convention on the Rights of the Child. Article 3 states: 'The best interests of the child must be a top priority in all decisions and actions that affect children.' Furthermore, Annika Saarikko, Finland's minister of family affairs and social services, one of six female ministers out of a cabinet of eleven said, 'This is not about the mother's right or the father's right – but the child's right to spend time with both parents.'

At the moment of my employer's revelation (three weeks prior to our first child's due date!) that I was not entitled to enhanced pay as a biological father at my place of work, we were gobsmacked. We wrongly and naively expected to be treated with parity to birth mums. The reasons given were twofold. We assumed equality for any parent who elects to be the primary caregiver, and secondly (we later found out) the Shared Parental Leave policy was being appealed against at an upcoming Court of Appeal and we were hanging on the coat tails of 'In Capita Customer Management Ltd v Ali' and 'Hextall v Chief Constable of Leicestershire Police'. Both cases challenged that the two respective biological fathers were being discriminated against based upon their sex. In a baffling and utterly equality-defying decision, the Court of Appeal held that employers that enhance maternity pay for biological dads do not discriminate on the grounds of sex (either directly or indirectly) against employees who are offered shared parental leave paid at lower or statutory rates. They justified this ignorance by saying that mums need to be at home to breastfeed and as mentioned, it is imperative that they are the sole nurturer for the baby. Nobody seemed to consider A) this breastfeed-shames the bottle fed/combination of milk and bottled formula/or expressed breast milk birth mums, and B) dads are innately incapable of nurturing their baby!

In September 2019, I attended an Employment Tribunal Hearing (more details of the ridiculousness to follow later), where I claimed I experienced sex discrimination when my employers refused to offer me enhanced pay on par with adoptive parents and birth mums. We lost unanimously, which followed the aforementioned Court of Appeal decision. A smorgasbord of archaic drivel, completely detached from the needs of contemporary parenting. That is not just my specific view way up here on my high horse, if you compare the current 'Great' British institutionalised legal and bureaucratic nonsense to that of our Scandinavian cousins, particularly the folks over in Sweden and Iceland, our cousins who value their citizens' welfare and health above their Gross Domestic Product. Ah, Utopia.

A best-case scenario from sharing our experience of challenging the institutionalised stereotypes of parenting is a metaphorical call to arms for anyone who believes in the importance of equality in our society. Our dream objective was/is to create a positive and progressive legacy for the generations who follow. In doing so we hope the parental expectations in the UK will be refined in order to broaden the scope of equality to meet the needs of parents regardless of their gender, identity, and label.

As nice, common-sensical people, my wife and I were lured down the 'obvious' path where we have 'protected' rights as 'fortunate' members of an 'enlightened' western society. Turns out that this is utter bollocks down to its very core particle, where biological dads are concerned. Dads are like that person who people innately dislike and cannot explain why. There is something intangible about the unspoken need to restrict men from getting a leg up in society. After all, we have been the alpha throughout the world's history for forever and a day. Therefore, how very dare we ask for more. How dare we moan that we are not being treated as well as others?

How dare we identify ourselves as 'victims' when pointing out the truth that dads are treated less favourably than adoptive parents and birth mums? How dare we?

The UK's Equality Act 2010, which is literally written into our legal rights, is in place to protect nine characteristics from discrimination. These include – Age, Disability, Gender Re-assignment, Marriage, and Civil Partnership, Pregnancy and Maternity, Race, Religion or belief, *Sex* and Sexual Orientation. Seems cast iron and clear to me. As a UK citizen, I cannot be discriminated against as a result of my sex. Which begs the question as to how is it allowed and accepted as the norm to treat biological dads less favourably than our adoptive and birth mum counterparts. This unconscious, institutionalised bias against dads is in direct violation of the Equality Act 2010. Anyone who disagrees with this point is by definition a discriminator against biological dads. It's not a 'Yes, but…' scenario. Anyone who argues against my point is wrong, according to the literal protected characteristics set out within the act. An expression I will repeat later is that there has to be equality for all or there is no equality at all. Equality is a universal concept that takes a zero-tolerance approach against any form of discrimination.

But don't worry, the United Nations are there to fight against all forms of discrimination. The all-powerful, overarching guardian of planet Earth's morals. They will surely have our back. In 2015 (the same year that the UK introduced the flawed Shared Parental Leave policy, which treats biological dads less favourably that adoptive parents and birth mums) the U.N. introduced their comprehensive list of 17 Global Goals to make the world a better place by 2030. Global Goal Number Five is 'Gender Equality.' They state within: 'Gender bias is undermining our social fabric and devalues all of us.' Target 5.C of this goal goes on to share it will: 'Adopt and strengthen policies and enforceable legislation for gender equality.'

The good old knights of hope for the planet's future have also established the United Nations Convention for the Rights of the Child. After all, children are our future. A voice for children who would otherwise be mute and deprived of a clear and established voice is principally satisfying in terms of acting in a moral and all-encompassing manner. Lovely stuff. Specifically, Article 18 of the UNCRC states: 'A child or young person's parents will normally have the main responsibility for bringing them up. They should both do this, both share responsibilities, and both be concerned with the best interests of the child or young person in their care.'

Both parents. 'Both' being the key word used here. It does not point out that a mother has more rights to nurturing their child than a father does. Anyone else smelling a distinct odour of tokenistic bullsh*t where equality does not concern biological dads? In case you are still on the 'You're being a prissy Snowflake' side of the equality fence. Wrap your intellect around this.

As humans in a civilised society, we value our rights. Our 'Human Rights' if you want to put a label on it. Thankfully, the upper echelon of global government power players have established the Human Rights Act. Rights which some people have fought and lost their lives in order for others to benefit from. It states: 'In the United Kingdom, human rights are protected by the Human Rights Act 1998. Public authorities, like a local authority or the NHS, must follow the Act.'

Regarding my specific grievance, Article 14 of the Human

Rights Act 1998 relates to 'Prohibition of discrimination.'

My beef with the aforementioned global right for all human beings is that I work for a local authority, and I am a human, and I am being discriminated against because of my gender. This ridiculous 'Testicle Tax' is not only accepted by my employers. It also has the UK government's stamp of approval. And, nobody of power seems to acknowledge it, talk about it or challenge it. Bar a few of us dads, who are vocally challenging the forgotten role of the importance of a father, being an equal partner in raising and supporting their baby.

Thankfully, on a more local and closer to home level, and given that local authorities have to legally follow the articles within, the Human Rights Act 1998 is present at my employment. Hallelujah! I am a human being and an employee for a local authority and they helpfully celebrate how forward-thinking they are via their published values of how progressive and positive they are. Boom, there is hope. In addition, The Authority have an 'Equality and Diversity' policy to protect the several thousand employees who are dancing to their corporate tune under their bureaucratic brolly. Wait for it. Despite these 'Council Values' and their robust 'Equality and Diversity policy', I still lost our employment tribunal case for sex discrimination. A case that was based upon the disparity biological dads have in comparison to the more favourable provisions for adoptive parents and birth mums, and the application process for replying to my Shared Parental leave request taking thirteen weeks. Maternity Leave requests were taking six weeks to process and Adoption Leave requests took three weeks to process. Despite these cast-iron, unambiguous pillars of evidence, I unanimously lost my Direct Discrimination and Indirect Discrimination claims respectively. Unanimously. The judge and her two panel members all unanimously decided against my family; against all parents within the UK; against my employers' Council Values and Equality and Diversity policy; against Article 14 of the Human Rights Act 1998; against the UK's Equality Act 1998; the United Nations' Global Goals No.5, and the United Nations Convention for the Rights of the Child's Article 18.

A very big ruling by the judge. A very, very wrong ruling by the judge evidenced by the aforementioned tokenistic and hypocritical rights that marginalise biological fathers over and over and over and over and over and over again (six 'overs'). An unconstitutional decision which serves to reinforce the archaic stereotypes that underpin our social and moral fabric.

I am not a naïve bloke and prior to this (then grievance, now campaign) I was one of the most stress retardant people I have ever come across. For as long as I can remember I have valued an 'easy life' being nigh on at the top of my agenda. After all, ignorance can be bliss and stress is detrimental to our mental and physical health. It's science. I was all about that until a social injustice slapped me across the face. It is all too easy to ignore social injustices. It is far more appealing to religiously watch X-Factor. Or to pray for more likes on our holiday photos where we have detoxed on a juice diet to give a false importance to unimportance. Or, spend our money on a season ticket for our favourite football team. Or to obsess over how entertaining Anton and Bruno are on Strictly. Or downloading the Britain's Got Talent app. These are all distractions from what is actually the most important thing of all in the whole world. Family.

Family is the foundation of forming a child's belief system and moral compass for the rest of their lives, which in turn sets an example for their own children and so on and so forth. If a child could be born into family that sincerely adopts equality, where the old-school stereotypes of dads being the breadwinner and mums being the Nurturer no longer exist, what a brighter, socially equal future we will all have for the generations to come. It does not need to be any more complex than that.

We are dumbed down by society's 'distraction industry', and expected to keep well within our own lanes and not bother our little selves with the government's policies, which are established to control the masses. Nothing will ever change for the better if we do not care enough to challenge social injustices and change lanes when we recognise the importance of standing up for what is right.

'All right, Negative Nelly!' I hear some of you say. As with everything in life, there is a good and there is a bad. A Ying for every Yang. Taking on the 'Man' came with its pitfalls, as well as its benefits. People always wax lyrically about having a voice. I did not find mine for thirty-five years because I never needed it. I was the 'ignorance is bliss guy' remember. That was untill 'The Man' metaphorically hoofed me square in the bollocks when I was not looking and at the precise time when I needed support the most. Namely, Shared Parental Leave. More specifically, that I was not entitled to enhanced pay to fulfil my role as an equal partner in the nurture and care of our first child. And then, ladies and gentlemen and all other gender identity preferences, then I found my voice. And how! A passion awoke a giant within who I did not know existed. A giant who had always hibernated out of 'The Man's' way and minded my own business.

The easy option would have been to receive the

metaphorical toe-punt to my testes, roll over and to accept our fate subserviently. In doing so, concede that I was not deserving of an acknowledgement as a parent and unworthy of deserving the parity set in policy for adoptive parents and biological mums. I decided that as a parent I would always stand up for what is just and aspire to be the best possible role model for our daughter. If we had passively rolled over, I would always know that I fell at the first hurdle in being the role model I aspired to be. I felt particularly inspired to challenge the marginalisation of dads because of my employer's Equality and Diversity policy, which claims to challenge all discrimination for its employees. Moreover, The Authority claims to champion progressiveness, diversity and equality. The unconscious bias towards biological mums and adoptive parents was almost tangible and the stench of tokenism was almost unbearable at times.

The Shared Parental Leave policy was introduced in the UK in 2015 and is a Trojan Horse of discrimination against biological fathers. The politically correct façade appeared to give dads (partners) the opportunity to parent on par with the mums. Great, right? No. Firstly, as no enhanced pay is provided, only the wealthier families who can afford to take the financial hit and opt for dad (partner) to step into the stereotypical nurturing role of the caring mum, can do so. In our situation, my self-employed wife ideally wanted to return to work a few weeks after giving birth to our daughter and I would have taken the lion's share of leave to adopt the role of the elected primary caregiver. Unfortunately, with the statutory minimum pay being offered and with my wife being self-employed and the financial breadwinner in our home, it was not an affordable option for us.

Questions have been asked as to why the Shared Parental Leave uptake since its introduction has only been around 2% in the UK. Let's be honest. It does not take Miss Marple to work that one out, considering the disparity in financial provision and dads getting the sh*tty end of the stick. The institutional unconscious bias within the UK is incredibly evident culturally when you consider that the Shared Parental Leave uptake in Iceland currently is around 96% and ours is 2%. Let that sink in for a second. 'We are a long way from Reykjavik now, Toto!'

From the point of view of a biological father, me, the Shared Parental Leave policy demonstrates a blatant disregard for my civil rights, human rights and moral rights. A bit dramatic you think? Well, consider the following. Imagine I was a woman pointing out a clear and obvious disparity in her rights, in comparison to a man with more favourable rights. Now, imagine I was a woman with a disability pointing out how I was being discriminated against, as a man's rights were more favourable. What if I was a religious woman with a disability who was pointing out how a man is being treated far more favourably than me, because of their protected characteristic of having a penis and worshipping a different God? What if I was a religious, mentally ill, LGBTQQIAAP person from an ethnic minority community, with a physical disability and was being discriminated against by the men folk? Twitter would implode and there would be a mass pillaging of men and riots in the streets. In short, it would be a very teste time and men's heads would roll.

In order to fully paint the picture of who I am and where I come from, bear the following in mind. I am a heterosexual white male. In fourteen years of working with young people in my role within mid Wales as a substance misuse harm reduction worker and a youth justice prevention of offending case worker, I estimate that I have supported in the realms of over two hundred families over that time. I have only ever supported one young person who was of a mixed-race. Every other young person over that time have been white. I have only ever worked with one colleague who was of mixed-race. Bear with me, there is a point here. As a white, heterosexual, Welshman who has been raised in mid Wales, I have been lucky to have not been a victim of any inequality up until this grievance. Some would refer to me as being 'Male, heterosexual, able-bodied, white privileged.' This is relevant as I harbour a guilt for standing up against marginalisation because people who are not coming from a position of such privilege have experienced unconscious and conscious bias against them ever since they were old enough to recognise that they were being treated unfairly. Given that I have been and continue to be categorised by some as being privileged, some folks have referred to me as a 'Snowflake.' My understanding of such a label is that it is thrown at people who are unknowingly privileged within their life, are taking for granted how fortunate they are and are quick to moan and play the 'victim.' I disagree. I see a snowflake as someone who has the tenacity and will to stand up to the institution when they recognise ingrained prejudices. This guilt, is ridiculous, yet I struggle to completely shake it off. Why should I deserve to gripe about the system after only just encountering discrimination after three and a half decades of my life? When others have been discriminated against repeatedly throughout all of their lives. Woe is me.

Furthermore, in my unique professional situation, I have

supported hundreds of young people and their respective families throughout my career to date. At the core of this support is and has been a remit that promotes and celebrates positive moral attitudes and behaviours. I need to be the very embodiment of pro-social actions and am required to be a positive role model in order to be a moral template for a young person who is impressionable and surrounded by chaos. If I have any integrity at all, I have to act against prejudice to highlight the importance of morality. If I do not, then I would be a fraud. A faux moral celebrator. Projecting the unspoken hypocrisy of accepting that a biological dad deserves to be treated less favourably (see previous 'Testicle Tax' reference) than birth mums and adoptive parents. In short, I would be full of sh*t.

I conclude that unless there is equality across the board, then the very definition of equality is a moot point. Any challenge of social injustice is a worthy cause in my humble opinion. My grievance, if recognised and acted upon appropriately by the powers that be, will not only benefit all male biological fathers of every colour and ethnicity. It will also benefit the entire population of British families as a whole. A redistribution of parental rights will go a long way to achieve parental equality within every UK home, which will be a hugely positive and progressive step for a bright future. In a perfect world this would then be a benchmark for other people who feel discriminated against to challenge and by establishing a more enlightened culture, there will be more voices fighting against other examples of institutionalised unfairness.

Unfortunately, as things currently stand there is a wilful and wanton disregard for the rights of the biological father evidenced by the current bureaucratic gender bias which is entrenched within the fabric of our government institution. This has the negative knock-on effect of disempowering women's choice to return to the workplace after having a baby. They are expected to remain at home to nurture their offspring while the big guy earns them bucks.

There is unlikely to be a flood of dads excited to jump on my bandwagon, but at the very least they should be aware about their current lack of choice and rights with respect to parental provisions. The family should have the flexibility to tailor support to best suit their unique dynamic. There are no places for a 'Testicle Tax' or the 'Motherhood Penalty.' If there was financial parity and an acknowledgement of the unconscious stereotypical gender bias then, and only then, could WE as a society and THEY as bureaucrats have an honest crack at addressing the Gender Pay Gap and gender equality as a whole.

This whole palaver makes me genuinely infuriated because WE as humans ALL deserve to be free of discrimination in today's society. Equality for almost everyone is by its very definition an oxymoron. Unless there is equality for all, there is no equality at all.

What gives me the right to present this book? Surely it would be better for an esteemed professor or social scientist to determine an accurate depiction of marginalising biological fathers. Right? Well, some may think that and they may be correct. My justification for writing this book stems from me being a layperson with first-hand experience of the many pitfalls and the very few leg-ups in existence for the unnecessarily complex, unspoken, and ignored gender bias that exists within the UK, particularly in Wales and specifically at my county council. It is very important to point out that there are some progressive companies in Wales, such as the National Health Service (2019) and Welsh Government who have been offering enhanced pay for biological fathers on Shared Parental Leave. Private companies including Vodafone and Aviva also introduced equality for fathers and mothers who are on parental leave. There is hope and there is common sense in a few rare one-off cases.

With respect to contemporary Western life, there is a strong argument to say that our world is devoid of a moral conscience or any distinct structure of ethical guidance from all forms of publicised media. Therefore, it has never been so vital for humanity to be directed towards the light of righteousness by Human Rights and equality laws. They should be a rudder for us, and our world, to direct us towards social justice. In the absence of this rudder our current 'rights' are tokenistic and as useful as a pair of sunglasses to an owl. Collectively, the mass populous of us humans, are blindly suckling at the capitalist 'tweets' of Silicone Valley. Self-appointed slaves to the social media algorithms in an alternative post-modern simulation.

2
Protected Characteristics

'The difference between what we are doing and what we are capable of doing would solve most of the world's problems.'
  Mahatma Gandhi.

We have all heard of stereotypical gender labels. The origins appear to go all the way back to the bygone shenanigans of early cave people. The classic cave man 'hunter gatherer'. A champion of his ilk whose family is utterly dependent upon him to bring home the bacon (or woolly mammoth back in the day) appears to have been engrained in our conscious as an intrinsic part of our early primary school education. Here, the gender bias seeds are sewn for all young minds to germinate and sprout into an unconscious branded falsehood that males are predisposed to be the protector and provider, and the females are to be protected, provided for and remain within their cave to raise the children.

A label that I am more familiar with is that of the male 'breadwinner'. A similar principle to the caveman, just rebooted for a modern audience. The yang to this ying is the 'housewife'. Responsibilities focus on managing everything within the home, such as shopping, cooking, cleaning, and raising the Rug-Rats. The spiteful irony being that the sponges that are children soak up all of the information within their environment and the overwhelming compartmentalised gender expectations become one with the child's conscious. If this tired old merry-go-round continues, gender equality and an equal parental dynamic is doomed to keep rotating in a never ending cycle until a new method is recognised and adopted. Monkey see, monkey do.

To hone in closer to home, this is a convenient time to highlight 'Great' Britain's equality milestones. Let us take a moment to recognise how great we truly are. A 'United' Kingdom paints a beautiful image of a land where the people within are united together from the length and breadth of a bold, powerful and elite kingdom.

The Equality Act which came into force on 1st October 2010, as touched upon earlier, appears to be a fantastically progressive piece of legislation. It appears to champion a zero-tolerance stance on discrimination of any kind. Marvellous. Good old Blighty, a leading light for the civilized world. We might be little in comparison to other countries, but boy do we roll with a big ole swinging beam of hope. Here follows examples of successful legal discrimination claims against the nine protected characteristics for equality. A brand-new concept to me as I ventured on my calamitous way down the Employment Tribunal path was the notion of 'Hurt Feelings.' When considering potential outcomes to a case, you have to be mindful that there needs to be evidence of hurt feelings present for a claimant. If you have this, you have a basis by which a remedy can be established by the judge and their two legal aides who sit astride them like slices of justice on the honourable filling that is the judge. The following hurt feelings were judged upon via the most honourable filings in the land of united greatness that is Blighty.

Our legally protected characteristics are age, disability, gender re-assignment, marriage, and civil partnership, pregnancy and maternity, race, religion or belief, *sex* and sexual orientation.

In at number one is age.

Slater Gordon Lawyers website. 24 March 2016.

61-Year-Old Salesman Wins Age Discrimination Case.

A 61-year-old salesman nicknamed 'gramps' who was fired from his job selling wedding rings at Brown and Newirth has won his case for age discrimination.

Alan Dove, who had worked for the jewellers for 25 years, was awarded more than £63,000 in compensation after he brought an age discrimination and unfair dismissal case against his employer when his employment was terminated in April 2015.

Despite not being a grandfather, he was called 'gramps' by the head of the sales team, Gareth Thomas. Mr Thomas said he considered the nickname 'an affectionate term of address', but Mr Dove found it disrespectful and hurtful.

The Watford Employment Tribunal ruled that when Mr Dove was described as 'long in the tooth', 'old fashioned' and 'traditional' these were negative references to his age.

The tribunal said: 'Use of these phrases indicate views emanating from the customers which are negative views almost certainly based on the claimant's age.

'He was dismissed, in essence, because some of the clients that he was dealing with had been transferred to Mr Thomas by Mr Ball. This left, in Mr Ball's view, insufficient income to be generated by the claimant.'

Sadly, Mr Dove is not alone in experiencing unfair dismissal based on his age. Age discrimination can affect anyone in the UK regardless of what job you do. This case highlights an issue in the UK where people in their late 50s and early 60s are finding their careers being brought to an abrupt halt.

Mr Dove deserved to be treated better by the company where he worked his way up to the point where he was made responsible for middle England, South Wales and the Channel Islands.

There is no upper limit to compensation in cases where the unfair dismissal was because of a person's age. This is unlike normal unfair dismissal claims which are not discriminatory where there is a statutory cap on the compensation.

Compensatory awards are based on the individual's loss of earnings flowing from an unfair or discriminatory dismissal. In a discrimination claim, an individual may also be awarded a sum for injury to their feelings, which is based on how they have been affected by their treatment.

In at number two is disability.

Horler v Chief Constable of South Wales Police.

A police officer who was forced to retire from his job has won over £200,000 after an Employment Tribunal ruled that his employer had failed in its duties relating to his disability.

Mr Horler, a former police officer in the South Wales Police Service, made a claim for disability discrimination in the Employment Tribunal after he was dismissed from his role in the police service in December 2011 for the reason of redundancy. His problems in the police force started in 2009 after he started to suffer from pain and stiffness in one of his knees because of torn cartilage. He then developed arthritis and the South Wales Police Service accepted that he was disabled under the Equality Act 2010. After he was diagnosed he was placed on restricted back-office duties and in October 2010 Mr Horler was advised by occupational health that he would be unable to return to front-line duties because of his injury. He was then told that he would be unable to undertake "ordinary police duties" at a later date by a doctor and that he could consider applying for "ill-health" retirement. Mr Horler disagreed and was moved to a role as a camera room operator in 2011.

Later in 2011 Mr Horler was informed that the chief constable of the South Wales Police Service was recommending him for early retirement. Mr Horler was angered by this and submitted a grievance. He was then told that the positions in the camera room may be made redundant in the future. He was subsequently made redundant in December 2011.

The claim came to the Employment Tribunal earlier this year, with the Employment Tribunal ruling in Mr Horler's favour in his claim for disability discrimination. The Tribunal panel held that the police force had failed to make reasonable adjustments as such adjustments could have been made and there were a number of roles that would have been suitable for Mr Horler and that he had a reasonable chance of obtaining. Mr Horler was awarded £230,215 for injury to feelings and loss of earnings (as well as interest on these sums).

Chris Hadrill, an employment solicitor at Redmans, commented on the case: "This is one of two large awards stretching into the hundreds of thousands of pounds in the Employment Tribunal that were reported last week. Employers must be careful to try and take reasonable steps to consider suitable alternative employment for employees if they are making those employees redundant or believe that employee is no longer able to adequately perform that role because of age or disability. A failure to do so can lead to potentially expensive and time-consuming Employment Tribunal claims."

In at number three is gender re-assignment.

Primark faces £47k bill for 'shocking' transgender discrimination

Personnel Today by Ashleigh Webber on 13 Feb 2018.

An employment tribunal has told Primark to adopt a policy on how to deal with transgender staff after it found an employee was discriminated against in relation to gender reassignment.

Retail assistant Alexandra de Souza E Souza was constructively dismissed from her position at Primark's Oxford Street (West) store after being harassed for being transgender.

The store failed to deal with the matter appropriately, which the employment tribunal found amounted to direct gender reassignment discrimination. She was awarded £47,433.03 in compensation to cover injury to feelings and loss of pay and pension contributions.

De Souza E Souza informed Primark that she was transgender when she applied for a role in August 2016.

Her birth name – Alexander – appeared on her passport, but she told the interviewer that she would like to be called Alexandra.

The interviewer said the company had to use her official name for pay, but she could use whatever name she liked on her name badge.

Before she began the role, HR staff erroneously changed the preferred first name on the company's IT system from Alexandra to Alexander, and her title from Miss to Mr. This error was printed on her name badge and daily allocation sheets that were handed to supervisors on the shop floor.

Despite using her preferred name for a number of weeks, a supervisor began calling her Alexander and laughed when she was corrected.

Other staff also subjected her to unfair treatment on the basis of her gender identity. She alleged that staff sprayed men's perfume over her till until she started coughing, said she had "a man's voice", made comments about her sexuality, and called her "evil" and "a joke".

Complaints were made about the way other employees had treated her, including an incident when a colleague claimed there were "no ladies" in the female toilets when an electrician needed access, despite de Souza E Souza being there.

She claimed she was bullied out of a job that suited her and the discrimination had made her insecure about her gender identity. She said she was unable to return to work for some time and had developed panic attacks.

Judge Lewis said: "All this may well have been prevented had there been proper systems from the outset to preserve confidentiality for transgender employees. We find it shocking that the respondents could not devise a way of keeping the claimant's legal name off the core allocation sheets and out of the knowledge of her supervisors.

"The respondents ought to have been able to devise a system whereby only one or two people in HR and payroll were aware of the claimant's transgender status."

The employment tribunal recommended that by 31 March Primark should: adopt a written policy on how to deal with new or existing staff who are transgender or who wish to undergo gender reassignment include a reference to the existence of a policy of confidentiality in regard to transgender new starters in training materials for managers amend the materials used for equality training of staff, management and HR to include, if not already there, references to transgender discrimination ensure that transgender discrimination and harassment is referred to in all of its equality and harassment policies, along with any other protected characteristics under the Equality Act 2010 add into the training materials for management on handling grievances.

A spokesperson for the retailer, which is owned by Associated

British Foods, said: "Primark is an equal opportunities employer and we do not tolerate discrimination of any kind, against any person, on any grounds. All policies relating to our people are based on fair treatment for all, to ensure the promotion and practice of equality of opportunity.

"We are extremely disappointed that on this occasion, our usual high standards in implementing these policies were not met and we sincerely apologise to the employee in question for this.

"We remain fully committed to equal opportunities and are reviewing our internal policies and training to ensure similar issues do not arise in the future."

In at number four is marriage and civil partnership.

A heterosexual couple have won their legal bid for the right to have a civil partnership instead of a marriage.

BBC News. (27 June 2018)

The Supreme Court unanimously ruled in favour of Rebecca Steinfeld, 37, and Charles Keidan, 41, from London.

The court said the Civil Partnership Act 2004 - which only applies to same-sex couples – is incompatible with the European Convention on Human Rights.

Ms Steinfeld said she hoped the government does the "right thing" and extends civil partnerships to all.

"We are feeling elated," she told the BBC outside court. "But at the same time we are feeling frustrated the government has wasted taxpayers' money in fighting what the judges' have called a blatant inequality."

The judgement does not oblige government to change the law, although it does make it more likely that the government will now act, the BBC's legal correspondent Clive Coleman explained.

In a civil partnership, a couple is entitled to the same legal treatment in terms of inheritance, tax, pensions and next-of-kin arrangements as marriage.

The couple, who met in 2010 and have two children, said the "legacy of marriage" which "treated women as property for centuries" was not an option for them.

"We want to raise our children as equal partners and feel that a civil partnership - a modern, symmetrical institution - sets the best example for them," they explained.

Since March 2014, same sex-couples can choose whether to enter a civil partnership or to marry. This has not been possible for mixed-sex couples, which led Ms Steinfeld and Mr Keidan to argue that the law was discriminatory.

This ruling overturns a previous judgement made by the Court of Appeal, which rejected the couple's claim, in February of last year.

The judges ruled that current UK law was "incompatible" with human rights laws on discrimination and the right to a private and family life.

Announcing the court's decision, Lord Kerr said the government did not seek to justify the difference in treatment between same-sex and different sex couples.

"To the contrary, it accepts that the difference cannot be justified," he said.

LGBT and human rights campaigner Peter Tatchell called the ruling a "victory for love and equality".

"It was never fair that same-sex couples had two options, civil partnerships and civil marriages, whereas opposite-sex partners had only one option, marriage," he said.

In at five is pregnancy and maternity.

Employee called a 'baby farmer' was unfairly dismissed,

tribunal rules.

(26 Feb 2019 By Francis Churchill. People Management website)

An employee who was referred to by a colleague as a "baby farmer" after she returned from maternity leave was unfairly dismissed, a tribunal has ruled.

A Leicester employment tribunal found that Miss L Hayman had faced direct sex discrimination and harassment based on protected characteristics on specific occasions in her role at logistics firm Pall-Ex.

The tribunal also heard how Hayman was shouted at and faced "bullying behaviour" from her line manager, Mr Tancock, with one incident leaving the claimant in tears in the bathroom.

The judges said the "baby farmer" comment constituted less favourable treatment, and that the bullying behaviour Hayman faced contributed to a breach of the implied terms of trust and confidence in Hayman's contract.

In at six is race.

Gay black police officer wins discrimination case.

(Guardian. February the 20th 2012. @BenQuinn75)

Detective constable Kevin Maxwell had sued the Metropolitan police for race and sex discrimination.

A gay black police officer who accused Scotland Yard of racial and sexual discrimination has won his case at an employment tribunal, which also found that another officer deliberately leaked a "distorted account" of the claim to the Sun newspaper.

Detective Constable Kevin Maxwell, 33, sued the Met for race and sex discrimination after he was abused by colleagues while working in the counter-terrorism unit at Heathrow airport's terminal five.

Following a 36-day hearing in which Maxwell said he was used as a "buffer" when ethnic minority passengers were stopped at Heathrow, the Metropolitan police was heavily criticised by a judge at a Reading employment tribunal for failing to train officers to deal with ethnic minorities. The tribunal found that Maxwell was required to stop black and Asian people and then hand them over to white officers. It judged that his claim of direct racial discrimination was correct.

Maxwell said he had been subjected to harassment on the grounds of sexual orientation in March 2009 when a detective from Special Branch made comments in his presence about gay men.

A tribunal judge, Richard Byrne, said: "The tribunal makes the observation that it is very surprising – given the resources of the respondent [Metropolitan police] and a well-drafted reporting wrongdoing policy – that the respondent failed to train officers in the application of the policy and failed to comply with it on this occasion."

The panel was also told how Maxwell had been at a presentation at Paddington police station in London during which reference was made to a photograph of a man in a fairground surrounded by children and that he was "as gay as a gay in a gay tea shop."

Byrne said: "The comment having been made and other people in the room, including other supervisors, laughing and finding it amusing was inevitably conduct that a gay police officer would reasonably consider as having the effect of violating their dignity and creating an intimidating, hostile, degrading, humiliating or offensive environment for them."

Following the incidents, Maxwell went on extended sick leave but was said to have been treated dismissively by senior officers during this period.

When raised his concerns by telling told a chief inspector it was "difficult being black and gay", the senior officer said: "That's life". Byrne ruled this was direct discrimination on the grounds of race and sexual orientation, along with harassment.

Ruling on the claim by Maxwell's partner, Alex Parr, that details had been leaked to the Sun newspaper about the claims, Byrne said, "The tribunal is entirely satisfied on the evidence heard that on the balance of probabilities the information about the claimant's case acquired by the Sun came from an officer working for the respondent."

On this matter, a spokesperson for the Independent Police Complaints Commission confirmed it was supervising an investigation by the Metropolitan police directorate of professional standards into a complaint.

In this case, aspects of the Metropolitan Police were proven to be as homophobic as a homophobe in a homophobic Humble Pie Shop.

In at seven is religion or belief.

Rather than get bogged down in the semantics of popular, organised religions, I want to highlight two modern religious beliefs. That of the 'Jedi' and of 'Scientology'. The former is based upon the fictional science-fiction screenwriter George Lucas's ground-breaking movie franchise *Star Wars*. The latter is based upon the concepts of fictional science-fiction writer L. Ron Hubbard. Even with emerging 'religions' the puppeteers are male figure heads. Coincidence that the founders of said newbies are male? That ruddy patriarchal boogieman cannot seem to be shaken off! Pulling the strings of social control and order. Any free-thinking oppositional opinionated folks are punishable by eternal damnation, (or a fall in grace to Darth's dark side; or feeling the alleged/denied scientology wrath of confinement and humiliation and be sent to 'The Hole'). In a world before Netflix (BN), the traditional religious threat must have been terrifying. Post Netflix (PN), any newbies run the risk of being documented and scrutinised by unprecedented worldwide viewing figures and critiqued to within an inch of their conception.

Mr Lucas' sci-fi saga first hit our screens back in 1977 and the first Scientology Church was established in December 1953, by its founder Mr Hubbard. 'Jedi', as a religious movement, came into our social conscious in 2001 when 'they' urged followers to record their religion as 'Jedi' or 'Jedi Knight' or 'Jediism' on the national censuses of the English-speaking world.

According to Catherine Beyer, updated in April 26th 2019 in *'An Introduction to Jedi Religion for Beginners.'* (www.learningreligions.com):

'Jedi believe in the Force, a specific energy that flows through all things and binds the universe together. They also believe that humans can tap into or shape the Force to unlock greater potential. Many Jedi also view themselves as guardians of truth, knowledge, and justice, and actively promote such ideals.

'Followers of Jediism also follow The Jedi Code, which promotes peace, knowledge, and serenity. There are also 33 Jedi Teachings To Live By, which further define the effects of the Force and guides Jedi on basic practices. Most of these are rather practical and positive, focusing on mindfulness and insight.'

Now, as beliefs go, the Jediism principles are not too shabby by most common sense minded people's standards. The plot thickened when the Charity Commission rejected the Temple of the Jedi Order's application on basis that it is not a 'cogent and distinct religion'.

Alice Ross's article 'Jedi order fails in attempt to register as religious group' in The Guardian on December 19th, 2016.

A Star Wars-inspired organisation has failed to use the force of its arguments to convince the charity watchdog that it should be considered a religious organisation.

The Temple of the Jedi Order, members of which follow the tenets of the faith central to the Star Wars films, sought charitable status this year, but the Charity Commission has ruled that it does not meet the criteria for a religion under UK charity law.

The commission wrote that Jediism "lacks the necessary spiritual or non-secular element" it was looking for in a religion.

Kenneth Dibble, the Charity Commission's chief legal adviser, said: "The meaning of 'religion' in charity law has developed over many years and now encompasses a wide range of belief systems.

"The decisions which the commission makes on the extent of this meaning can be difficult and complex, but are important in maintaining clarity on what is and is not charitable."

The Temple of the Jedi Order, based in Beaumont, Texas, is recognised as a charitable or non-profit group by the US Internal Revenue Service. Last year the charity regulator in New Zealand rejected an application by another group for Jediism to be considered a religion for charitable purposes.

The Temple's website says it promotes "goodwill, understanding, compassion and serenity."

"We do not teach mystical powers or how to build lightsabers, we are not a dedicated Star Wars fan site, we are not affiliated with George Lucas or Disney and we are not for people who just want to wear a badge reading 'I'm a Jedi'," it says.

Brenna Cavell, 32, a psychologist and spokeswoman for the Temple, said the group was disappointed by the charity commission's decision. "We put a lot of work into the application and really did our best to illustrate why we do consider ourselves a religion and why we believe we do offer benefits not just to our members but also to the public at large," she said.

The Collins definition of a religion is 'A particular system of faith and worship.' Hmm. Well, that sounds a definitive response from the UK powers.

The plot thickens to a quick-sand like goo when considering the definition within the Scientology official website, which states, 'Scientology is "a religion that offers a precise path leading to a complete and certain understanding of one's true spiritual nature and one's relationship to self, family, groups, mankind, all life forms, the material universe, the spiritual universe and the Supreme Being".'

It says Scientology is not a 'dogmatic religion in which one is asked to accept anything on faith alone' and the ultimate goal is 'true spiritual enlightenment and freedom for all'.

Hmm, I guess one person's barbecue is another person's grill.

In relation to the Equality Act (2010), the article 'Supreme Court judges allow Scientology wedding', on the BBC News website, December 11th, 2013.

A woman who wants to marry in a Church of Scientology chapel has won her Supreme Court challenge.

Five Supreme Court judges ruled the church was a "place of meeting for religious worship".

Louisa Hodkin launched legal action after officials refused to register a Church of Scientology chapel in central London as a place for marriage.

This was due to a 1970 High Court ruling which said Scientology services were not "acts of worship".

<u>Evolution of beliefs</u>

In their unanimous decision, the Supreme Court justices said that the 1970 ruling's definition of religious worship as involving "reverence or veneration of God or of a supreme being" was out of date.

"Religion should not be confined to religions which recognise a supreme deity," wrote Lord Toulson, giving the judgment.

Victorious claimant Louisa Hodkin shared "We are really excited that we can now get married."

"To do so would be a form of religious discrimination unacceptable in today's society," he wrote, noting that the criteria would exclude Buddhism, among other faiths.

Although I find it confusing as to what the difference is between branding Scientology as a religion when Jediism cannot be, the protected characteristic of our religion or belief was successful in Louisa Hodkin's discrimination case at the Supreme Court. The highest court in our land.

In at eight is sex.

£3m Sex Discrimination case winner Ms Lokhova: 'Everybody loses'

(By Simon Cox BBC Radio 4's The Report. April 30th, 2015.)

'Toxic atmosphere' (When Ms Lokhova started HR new post at investment banking firm Sberbank CIB)

Crucially, however, some at Sberbank CIB's London office did not want her there as she had been appointed from head office.

Her new job was in a small, quiet office - and she immediately felt hostility from her new colleagues.

"The atmosphere was sort of strange and I started getting reports from people when I'm not in the office. People, especially my direct boss, calling me derogatory names."

Names like "Miss Bonkers" - but there was much worse being

said by her direct boss, David Longmuir, in emails and messages to her colleagues and clients in major investment banks.

"Crazy Miss Cokehead can have my desk," said one, calling her a "schizo nightmare... another expensive mistake".

Ms Lokhova did not know about these messages but the atmosphere was starting to affect her work.

"In the sales environment you have to be a very sort of happy person and very confident because it's actually very tough to call a very important client from scratch. You have to be in the right frame of mind."

She had worked hard to build a successful career in investment banking but says her confidence now began to drain away.

"This toxic atmosphere, it was getting me sort of quite upset. I thought I was just being paranoid, I thought I'm imagining [it] but I just felt really, really stressed."

By the end of 2011, just six months into her new post, Ms Lokhova complained to the bank that she was being discriminated against - a month later she was placed on sick leave by her doctor.

She tried to negotiate an amicable exit from the company. Her lawyer asked for any written communications about her. Several boxes arrived and Ms Lokhova was stunned at what she discovered.

On the first page was a message from her direct boss, David Longmuir, to a client, before she even arrived at Sberbank CIB (UK), which said: "We're all quaking here awaiting for arrival of a crazy Miss Cokehead in a puff of sulphurous smoke."

"I just remember opening the first page," says Ms Lokhova, "and everything just going blank and me just bursting into tears and dropping the file.

"My whole career flashed in front of me and to have somebody just basically just take it away from me like this, I just couldn't understand."

This case is wholly unfortunate as it leaves a bittersweet taste. I appreciate that the financial sector worker bees are not renowned for their selfless acts and to be successful it appears that they have to be of a harder nature than say a special needs primary school nature is. Having said that, they are humans too. The sweet taste is that Ms Lokhova won three million pounds for the breach of her protected characteristic of her sex by her employers in a remarkably immature and unprofessional way. The bitterness follows as Ms Lokhova shared that she spent the best part of the three million on the 'vulturistic' world of solicitors. Given the case involves a financial sector corporation the biggest sharks with the pointiest teeth and therefore largest fees would have been circling these waters. Hence, the title quote, 'Everyone loses.'

In at number nine is sexual orientation.
    Sexual Orientation Discrimination Case Settled for £30,000.
    (COOP Legal Services. 6th February 2017)
    An Employment Law Case Study.
    <u>Client Situation</u>

Mr R worked for his employer for over 5 years. He was an openly gay man and sometimes took part in friendly 'banter' around the office. However, things escalated when a new line manager started and made offensive comments to our client. Mr R felt offended by the comments and kept copies of emails sent to him on the work computer, in which he was called inappropriate names.

Mr R asked the line manager to stop making comments in an informal conversation but he continued. Comments were also made in the open plan office. The tipping point was when the line manager groped Mr R at a work function and made inappropriate sexual comments. Our client was too afraid to attend work after that incident and was signed off for anxiety and stress at work. Unfortunately, none of Mr R's colleagues would stand up for him. Mr R felt isolated and vulnerable as a result of his line manager's actions.

He called our Employment Solicitors for legal advice as he was worried no one would believe him and he was afraid to face his line manager. He was unsure whether to resign or what his rights were on sexual orientation discrimination and harassment.

How We Helped

Our Employment Lawyers advised Mr R on a fixed fee basis, initially providing half an hour telephone advice for £60 including VAT. He then instructed us to conduct a complex written investigation report for £840 including VAT setting out his options and legal rights. The matter was complex as we had to advise on sexual orientation discrimination and harassment claims. We advised him to raise a formal grievance against his line manager.

The employer delayed in dealing with the grievance and was unsupportive throughout the grievance investigation. Mr R's access to his work emails was suspended by his employer when he raised his grievance which we advised was an act of victimisation, and a further act of discrimination. Mr R's grievance was not upheld as they said that Mr R has participated in the 'banter' and therefore it was not unwanted conduct (harassment) or discrimination. We advised Mr R to appeal the grievance outcome, which he did.

Due to the limitation deadlines being imminent Mr R instructed us to lodge an Early Conciliation claim using our Negotiation Fixed Fee package at £300 including VAT. We lodged the Early Conciliation forms on his behalf and drafted a Letter Before Action. Several lengthy letters were exchanged between ourselves and Mr R's employer as they initially rejected our first offer to settle.

A commercial offer of £3,000 was made by Mr R's employer and evidence was exchanged between parties over a course of a month as part of heavy negotiations. This resulted in an increased offer of £9,000 from the employer. We continued to negotiate until we obtained £30,000 tax free settlement for our client.

The Outcome

Mr R was very happy with the tax free severance package of £30,000, five times the amount his employer first offered him. Mr R said that he was very grateful for her support during a very stressful time and impressed with her negotiation skills.

Mr R was able to move on and find work elsewhere in a better working environment.

I imagine Mr R was a very satisfied man because his human rights and his protected characteristic of sexual orientation was legally championed in an appropriate and common-sensical way. Ah, the sweet scales of justice, tipping in favour of progressiveness.

Conclusion of the nine protected characteristics.

Please do not interpret the following as flippant or ignorantly undermining the previously celebrated outcomes with regards to the range of protected characteristics. I want to point out the 'hurt feelings' caused by the respondents to the claimants and the rulings established to make amends. Furthermore, I am going to bluntly highlight the outcomes by presenting an unencumbered and clear comparison of the protected characteristics to that of my grievance with my protected (failure to protect) characteristic of my sex with regards to being a biological dad. My overall aim is to highlight the importance of a blatant and confusing chasm present for us biological dads. Here goes:

A sixty-one-year-old man's feelings were hurt when his manager and colleagues called him names such as 'Gramps', 'long in the tooth', 'old fashioned,' and 'traditional'. It was deemed that he was discriminated against because of his protected characteristic of age. He was awarded a sum of £63,000.

Concerning disability, police officer Mr Horler was awarded £230,215 for injury to feelings and loss of earnings (as well as interest on these sums). It was not only his feelings that were injured. His bad knee was the catalyst for his sheer presence being a perceived pain in the proverbial arse for his employers, who were judged to have failed to make reasonable adjustments to accommodate Mr Horler. By making him redundant, they discriminated against the claimant because of said bad knee.

Retail assistant Alexandra de Souza E Souza was constructively dismissed from her position at Primark after being harassed for being transgender.

The store failed to deal with the matter appropriately, which the employment tribunal found amounted to direct gender reassignment discrimination. She was awarded £47,433.03 in compensation to cover injury to feelings.

Protected characteristic number four is marriage and civil partnership. Here a heterosexual couple argued that they should be allowed to choose whether they get married or have a civil partnership. They wanted the title on their union contract and big day invitations to be 'Civil Partnership'. This was based upon the 'legacy of marriage' which 'treated women as property for centuries' was not an option for them as they wanted to raise their children as equal partners and felt that 'a civil partnership – a modern, symmetrical institution – sets the best example for them.' These views dove-tail perfectly with my argument of parents being an equal team. To quote Mr Robert Dylan, 'The times, they are a-changing.' At a slower rate in the UK than in comparison to the more progressive nations, such as over in Scandinavia.

Since March 2014, same sex-couples can choose whether to enter a civil partnership or to marry. This has not been possible for mixed-sex couples, which led Ms Steinfeld and Mr Keidan to successfully argue that the law was discriminatory. Perhaps the first building block in creating an equal parental partnership. Here's hoping.

Number five, was the 'baby farmer!' Of the list provided, my favourite quote as it completely highlights an example of discriminative ridiculousness. The judges said the 'baby farmer' comment constituted less favourable treatment, and that the bullying behaviour Hayman faced contributed to a breach of her contract. When I first read this, I immediately visualised her manager as Finchy from *The Office*. How some people rise to positions of management absolutely baffles me.

The sixth protected characteristic was race. Detective Constable Kevin Maxwell's case versus the Met's counter-terrorism unit at Heathrow also included sex discrimination. He was used as a 'buffer' to liaise with ethnic minority passengers at the airport because he was black. The additional kicker was that he was then expected to hand them over to white officers.

Maxwell said he had been subjected to harassment on the grounds of sexual orientation in March 2009 when a detective from Special Branch made comments in his presence about gay men. A reference was made to a photograph of a man in a fairground surrounded by children and that he was 'as gay as a gay in a gay tea shop'. The audience, including other supervisors, were tickled pink by this and had a right good giggle at the expense of sexual orientation discrimination.

When raising his concerns by telling a chief inspector it was 'difficult being black and gay', the senior officer said: 'That's life.' Well, it is life, Chief Inspector, but not as we know it, or accept it to be.

The seventh protected characteristic successfully challenged was religion and belief. Five Supreme Court judges ruled the church was a 'place of meeting for religious worship'. Louisa Hodkin launched legal action after officials refused to register a made-up Church of Scientology chapel as a place for marriage. In their unanimous decision, the Supreme Court justices said that the 1970 ruling's definition of religious worship as involving 'reverence or veneration of God or of a supreme being' was out of date. Lord Toulson who gave the judgement stated that, 'Religion should not be confined to religions which recognise a supreme deity'. Victorious claimant Louisa Hodkin shared: 'We are really excited that we can now get married.' It appears that the force was strong within Louisa's argument. Just to reiterate, L Ron Hubbard was not a messiah, evidenced by him not performing any miracles that have been reported. He was a sci-fi writer with such publications as Battlefield Earth, and The Automagic Horse. He passed away in 1986 and thanks to Louisa Hodkin's case his legacy within the UK is that a building labelled as a Church of Scientology chapel of his made-up Scientology movement is now recognised as a religious building capable of legal marriage. Be patient Jediism. Now may not be your time but maybe in a galaxy, far, far away you are being recognised as a legitimate religion.

The penultimate protected characteristic of the Equality Act is 'Sex' and the case of investment banker Ms Lokhova.

She experienced what she perceived to be a strange work atmosphere at her new job and started hearing rumours that her boss was calling her nasty names, such as 'Miss Bonkers'. The strange atmosphere and nasty names pushed her to her limit after just six months into her new job, she complained to the bank that she was being discriminated against, and a month later she was signed off by her doctor.

After unsuccessfully negotiating an amicable exit her lawyer requested all written communications regarding her. This was when the shit proverbially hit the fan when the correspondence (unknown by Ms Lokhova) revealed that her boss had referred to her in emails to clients and colleagues as 'Crazy Miss Cokehead can have my desk,' he also called her a 'schizo nightmare... another expensive mistake'. Ball well and truly dropped by her male boss. Her boss called her nasty words. Result being, a three million pound pay out. The irony being that the legal fees costed her three million quid too. With regards to a successful remedy for the claimant, there wasn't one. The slick, gooey dance of solicitors versus investment banking was a marriage made in limbo.

Finally, number nine is sexual orientation. An openly gay man who 'sometimes' took part in friendly 'banter' (Banter has become a trip-wired minefield, given the spectrum of acceptability we all sit within) in an open plan office. The bants took a turn for the worse when the claimant's line manager took up the banter baton and made offensive comments to a client. The Bantersaurus Rex was asked to stop but continued nonetheless. The line-manager showed that he was devoid of any respectability, common sense or nous when he exacerbated the toxic scenario by groping the claimant and making inappropriate sexual comments. The name calling and groping was judged so hurtful to the claimant that he sought legal representation, won his case, and received a £30,000 remedy.

'The previous nine cases are examples of how we all have an iron clad custodian of righteous protection from our protected characteristics within the bureaucratic marvel that is, the Equality Act 2010.' – Baz Price.

That is what I would have said if it was entirely true. However, there is a significant, ignored and blatantly sexist caveat, to the apparent virtuous and morally balanced Equality Act. Namely, the embedded biological dad 'testicle tax', which is being brushed under the proverbial progressive carpet. Evidenced by the fact that biological dads are only entitled to basic, minimum statutory pay on the only parental leave provision available, the Shared Parental Leave policy of 2015. Our 'protected' characteristic of sex is ignored, as birth mums and adoptive parents are offered enhanced pay in recognition of their roles as nurturing parents. Dads are literally the poor relation in this scenario.

Despite the apparent zero tolerance to discrimination within the Human Rights Act, Equality Act, United Nations Global Goal 5, United Nations Convention for the Rights of the Child, and my employer's council values and Equality and Diversity policy, dads are not given an equal or proportionate recognition within the role of parenting. This makes a mockery of the protection of dads' human rights and protected characteristic of sex. The hypocrisy, tokenism and misandry is a stinking great elephant in the room of equality. A system which has been historically rigged in favour of white, male heterosexual patriarchs are the devil. Perched with our pitch-forks in hand, at the summit of our oppressive throne ever since '*man* was created in the image of God'.

To quote the brilliant Douglas Murray in his book *The Madness of Crowds*, 'the rules are made up not by rational people, but by mob stampedes. Rather than derange ourselves by working out a puzzle that cannot be solved, we should instead try to find ways out of this impossible maze.' This quote resonates with me and my family's situation because the answer appears to be blatantly obvious and yet the journey to the answer is a quest akin to completing a Rubik's Cube, blindfolded, sat in a bath of treacle and being thrown out of an aeroplane at 30,000 feet. When it should be a ramble down a very short and gentle slope with a cwtch, a cuppa and a slice of sponge waiting for me at the destination. Addressing discrimination which underpins the expectations of every family within the United Kingdom should have been completed decades ago. Why in 2020 the blindness, ignorance and acceptance of a dad's allocated parental lot is beyond my little mind. The 'mob stampede' have/are shouting about every other perceived injustice while ignoring dad's rights to perform as an equal within a parental dynamic.

At the conception of each and every landmark was someone's realisation of an unconscious bias occurring, followed by a catalyst involving someone taking a stand. And like dominoes, the failings in social justices toppled and climaxed in a righteous collapse. Like a moral phoenix rising from the persecuted ashes, a social justice is born.

Out of the nine protected characteristics within the Equality Act (2010), why is there a granite wall stopping biological fathers from challenging their marginalised rights in parenting based upon our sex? I use the word 'biological' again as if I was a gay man who wanted to adopt a child with my male civil partner, for example, then I could benefit from the more 'fashionable' protected characteristics of sexual orientation and civil partnership. Therefore, I could take advantage of the more favourable provisions within the Adoption Leave policy which does offer enhanced pay on par with that of birth mums on maternity leave. Where are our protected rights? Why are we institutionally marginalised? Why the reluctance of legal institutions such as the Employment Tribunal, Employment Appeals Tribunal, Court of Appeal, and Supreme Court to commit to the protected rights established unequivocally in the Human Rights Act (1998) and the Equality Act (2010).

In brief, my takeaway is that Colin from Scarborough who wants to be a Jedi Warrior has more legal importance than a biological dad.

3
So what is this Shared Parental Leave policy all about?

'If you want to change the culture, you will have to start by changing the organization.'
    Mary Douglas.

On paper, this sounds like the Holy Grail of equality for contemporary families who want an equal partnership to parental responsibilities. It reads very progressively and in keeping with the desire for gender equality. When I first heard my employers had this provision available, my expectant wife and I were pleasantly impressed with them and were keen as the proverbial beans. Unfortunately, when it comes to running a business, some employers, despite the bloated salaries of their big-wigs, still have not worked out that you cannot outsource staff morale and you cannot morally launder the treatment of their employees by washing it with non-bio 'spin' detergent. A cavalier attitude towards accountability and the implementation of a zero-tolerance approach to the discrimination of its employees, will destroy any hope of giving staff the notion that they are valued and working towards a positive future. It does not take Professor Brian Cox to determine that if you invest in the wellbeing and enablement of a workforce you will reap the rewards of greater productivity, reduced levels of sickness leave, improve job retention, and create a more inclusive and diverse labour force. Oh yeah, it would also be the right and ethical path to choose.

But (and it is a big but), the Shared Parental Leave policy is fundamentally flawed in my humble opinion. I can evidence this on two counts. Firstly, unlike Maternity Leave in all employment and Adoption Leave in some employment, the Shared Parental Leave policy does not offer enhanced pay. Secondly, it includes a grey lottery area which states 'some employers offer enhanced pay.' So, if you can afford to take the financial hit or you are lucky enough to work for one of the employers who offers enhanced pay then you are good to go. But, what about the parents who cannot afford to take the financial hit and do not have a progressive employer? Welcome to our predicament.

The Shared Parental Leave policy was introduced in the UK in 2015 and parents are eligible if your child was born on or after 5th April 2015. For all you parents acquainted with CBeebies and 'Go Jetters', here are some funky facts for you.

Eligible parents can share up to fifty weeks of leave and up to thirty-seven weeks of pay between them.

A study conducted by the TUC (The Trade Union Congress' website shares that they bring together more than 5.5 million working people who make up our forty-eight member unions. Tagline, 'Changing the world of work for good') reveals that, unfortunately, of the more than 900,000 UK parents who were eligible for Shared Parental Leave in 2018, only 9,200 parents made use of it. That is somewhere in the region of 1% of the eligible parents.

Could awareness be the issue? A survey conducted by employment website Monster.co.uk found that 50% of UK employees are unaware whether their company even offers shared parental leave.

46% of UK employees said that employers should promote Shared Parental Leave to encourage more men to participate in the program and drive gender equality forward in the workplace (sourced from *info.benify.co.uk*).

In case you have not come to your own conclusion about my specific set of skills (or lack thereof) regarding a plausible challenge to the flawed Shared Parental Leave policy, I have sourced evidence from the brightest and most relevant minds the World Wide Web can muster throughout this book. The following is a quote from Raoul Parekh, a partner at specialist employment law firm GQ|Littler. They succinctly and clearly highlight the foibles of the policy within the online article 'Why it's time to rethink shared parental leave' in *www.peoplemanagement.co.uk* on 12 Nov 2018:

'There are three easy policy moves the government should make.

'First, extend SPL by 12 weeks, but reserve the period solely for fathers. Then mothers wouldn't have to give up their maternity leave to return to work early to enable fathers to spend time at home. Keeping the existing 52 weeks means that when a mother does return early, there is scope for the father to be at home instead.

'Second, pay for those 12 weeks on (at least) the same terms as maternity leave – with employers able to reclaim the cost from HMRC in the same way. This would remove the enormous pay penalty facing all fathers whose employers do not choose to top up the low statutory pay levels. Without this move, most families will simply not be able to afford to have two parents at home simultaneously. It's also fair that the cost of furthering our common gender equality goals is spread across society and not concentrated solely on employers.

Finally, this time, run the publicity campaign when the new rights are created: don't wait three years for people to notice.'

It is hard to read such articles without comparing the UK's tepid approach on parental rights to that of the fantastisk manner of the Swedish and other Scandinavian countries. I feel like the commitment of my employers in mid Wales are less Swede and more Turnip. Money is never as tight as when you are supporting a family. Therefore, if the pay for dads, such as myself, is less than that of a mum on Maternity Leave then the Shared Parental Leave policy is doomed to fail. Unless you can afford to take the hit in your wages. Which begs the question, where is the equality in that? Both from a financial and gender point of view.

The Court of Appeal, in its innovative and infinite wisdom, judged in two sex discrimination claims by biological fathers in May 2019, that 'Fundamentally, the Court concluded that maternity leave fulfils a range of different purposes to SPL, for example to allow mothers to recuperate from the effects of childbirth and to develop the special relationship between the mother and the new-born child. In doing so, the Court rejected the contention that the predominant purpose of both SPL and maternity leave is to facilitate childcare.' (www.dacbeachcroft.com)

Now, if we just pull over, park up for a second and mull this judgement over. Here is why I find this pill a hard one for us to swallow. Speaking as a dad, and dare I say, my thoughts might be echoed by one of the dozens of other identities parents embrace too, this 'develop the special relationship' is undeniably vital in a baby's attachment to a parent. How in good conscience can the COA play the moral God role of deciding that it is solely the birth mother's right to attain this higher power when all of us parents, who do not identify as the birth mother, do not have such a right allowed to us as well. Not instead of, but as well as.

I want to make it abundantly clear that birth mums need the time to recuperate both physically and psychologically from pregnancy and childbirth. Nobody in their right mind would argue against this. The grey area for me raises its curious head when I consider the following relating to birth-mum from www.gov.uk which states, 'You do not have to take 52 weeks but you must take 2 weeks' leave after your baby is born (or 4 weeks if you work in a factory).'

So by my reckoning, if a mum returns to her job after two weeks (or four weeks if she works in a factory setting) of having given birth, her partner, the birth father, would not be entitled to the more favourable terms of pay that are present within the Maternity Leave policy, if he accesses the only other parental provision available to him, Shared Parental Leave. So, mum would have continued to have been paid the more favourable terms if she had not gone back to work. Dad however, would not be entitled to the same provisions in order to develop the special relationship between himself and their new-born child. Even though mum has made the decision, that she has recuperated and recovered enough to return to work. How fantastic would it be if the birth mums who have a present co-parent could access their support in order to recuperate and fulfil their work-life balance desires and career goals?

I have every hope that back in the pre Brexit and pre Covid-19 days, the Shared Parental Leave plan was well intended in playing a significant role in gender equality concerning parenting and labour force opportunities. Unfortunately, it appears that 'the powers that be', failed to foresee the flaws that were lying in wait. Or a more cynical mind may surmise that this was just one big ole box ticking exercise and a short-sighted, tokenistic veneer to appear like an all-singing, all-dancing progressive government. When in fact, there never was the absolute commitment to meet the contemporary needs of modern families via a solid foundation and weight-bearing scaffolding established to incorporate the permanent pillars within.

Regrettably, some more insular companies failed to embrace the ajar door and maintained their tokenistic micro cultures, who at first glance look ethically upstanding but scratch under the surface and you soon discover a symbolic effort to keep up inclusive appearances without implementing actual workforce provisions. In parallel with hollow words is the feet dragging until the government wakes up and literally alters the policy's stance from leaving it up to the 'some employer's' moral compass as to whether they offer enhanced pay for their respective workforce, to stating that 'all employers' will pay their workforces enhanced pay.

A new study, which looked into the parental leave policies of 200 large companies, has found that just three firms offer the same amount of time off to both parents.

The research from Equileap, a company that provides data on gender equality, named drinks giant Diageo, which owns Smirnoff, Baileys, and Guinness; insurance firm Aviva; and finance company Investec as the best for giving their staff equal parental leave.

According to Diana van Maasdijk, chief executive at Equileap, it is this lack of transparency from employers that causes the so-called 'motherhood penalty' – maternity discrimination which sees women who have had children by the age of thirty-three earning 15% less than their peers who remained childless.

'Sadly, not many companies are offering equal opportunities for men and women when it comes to maternity and paternity leave, with most offering just a couple of weeks to men,' van Maasdijk said.

'A strong paternity package is essential to create equality in the workplace. At the moment, it is nearly always the responsibility of a woman to take time out of their career for children whether they want to or not.'

The findings follow a 2018 study which found that an increasing number of dads crave further access to paternity leave, called 'Helping Dads Care'. The report from Dove Men+Care and Promundo – an organisation which promotes gender equality – revealed that a growing number of men would like to be more involved in the early weeks and months after the birth of their child.

Excellent right? Another shining light on a gender-neutral polar shift. Pump the brakes for second. It was reported that of the 250 FTSE (The Financial Times Stock Exchange, also known as the 'Footsie', is a share directory to gauge the prosperity of capital on the London Stock Exchange) only fifteen firms publicise their parental leave policies.

On Nov 19th, 2019, Ashleigh Webber reported in 'Personnel Today':

'Only 15 of the organisations in the FTSE 250 are telling job candidates how much paid leave they could expect if they have a baby, according to new analysis.

'Parents' network Mumsnet, which looked at which of the organisations published their parental leave policies on their websites, found that FTSE 250 firms were more likely to tell potential candidates about the availability of perks such as fresh fruit or massage therapy than the levels of leave and pay they would be entitled to if they became a parent.'

So, still a long way to go, many would say. When perks such as a shiny bushel of Granny Smiths and an Indian Head Massage appear to be prioritised over parental leave provisions, some may say, 'Dads, you're screwed!'

4
Equality Landmarks

The word misandry was a brand new word to me. You too? 'Misogynist' is a well-known word and I am aware of it as far back as I can remember. But misandry? I did not have a Scooby. Thirty-six years and I have never come across it. Misandry is defined as 'Hatred of men'. Now I know what it means, it is obvious why. As a guy, since raising my hand to highlight the marginalisation of dads, I have been cautious of a potential mob stampede. Given how I am a member of the patriarchal society, discrimination is and has always been one sided to the detriment of everyone apart from men. Particularly white, wealthy, heterosexual men. Therefore, I totally understand that I am a little voice screaming into a hurricane and my grievance towards sex discrimination is a tiny anecdote in the vast overall narrative. Despite this, it is still undeniable inequality and discrimination by the very definition of the word – 'Equality is the same status, rights, and responsibilities for all the members of a society.' Whatever viewpoint you may have on parental leave provision, the anchoring centre point is this clear and unambiguous definition.

Our grievance is somewhat Shrek-like because it is layered, in that I am not saying that the collateral damage shrapnel of this inequality is just imbedded in us dads alone. It is embedded within contemporary parents who want to be partners in the care and upbringing of their children. The benefit of parity in parental provisions will serve as a ripple effect that will wash over society as a whole, setting a progressive example in the foundation of our children's view of their world. It appears to be nigh on impossible to decipher the rules of the 'Equality Game of Life.' Differing rules are adopted, dependent upon the stock and shareholders of each of the nine protected characteristic narratives within the Equality Act (2010). It appears that either you can surrender to the notion that it is time for the dad-folk to accept and adopt their new downtrodden identity. Or, we can all come out all tweets blazing and hashtag the bejesus out of the apparent misandry injustice. Like a keyboard-warrior attempt at replicating the doomed shootout in the finale of Butch Cassidy and the Sundance Kid. Or use indisputable evidence which reflects an honest contemporary narrative from the perspective of a biological father being held hostage by bureaucratic bollocks which supersedes human rights, equality and diversity policies, and protected characteristics. No 'conquer and dividing' or adopting the age old 'Us vs Them' perpetual societal control strategy. Just honesty and unhindered clarity.

My experience of representing myself at the Employment Tribunal, on behalf of all biological fathers and our alleged protected characteristic of sex, left me feeling like I had been whacked by the mafia and buried in an unmarked grave in the woods for daring to disrespect the reputation of the mob.

Out of the 9 protected characteristics why is there a granite wall stopping fathers from challenging their marginalised rights in parenting based upon their sex?

A desired and deserved utopia is left very much wanting, given the stark reality.

By collecting allies, we just perpetuate the cycle of conflict instead of positively rejoicing in mutual equality for all parents of all protected characteristics.

The positives are there in black and white. Equality Act, Human Rights, United Nations Global Goals, United Nations Convention for the Rights of the Child. Free speech is a contentious paradox. Nothing is free in this world. Concessions are expected to be made to banish hate speak in order to prevent unacceptable alienation. Bar a few tokenistic glitches in the bureaucratic matrix, the UK is a stellar place to live and thrive. Safe in the knowledge that if we blow that whistle, or make a formal complaint, there are procedures in place to air our grievances without the fear of being kidnapped and holed up in a George Orwellian *1984* type nightmarish reality.

With specific acknowledgement in my personal tale, to the censorship via the Social Media policy at my place of work, presented in later chapters, the murky waters of authoritarian dictatorship present themselves at their most sketchy with the directive that reinforces that any employee who 'brings the council into *disrepute*' (with the council being judge, jury, and executioner based on how they interpret if disrepute has occurred in their opinion) can have their contracts terminated because of a perceived gross misconduct. Therefore, if an employee makes an honest and factual remark online with no malice or hate, they can be disciplined or sent packing down the road to the Job Centre. Even if an employee mentions the council by name in a Change.org petition, they could be disciplined or sent packing. Even if an employee shares or comments on another person's online petition, they can risk disciplinary action. True story. More specifics to my story to follow in later chapters, including bullying and harassment from senior management towards me for expressing how disgruntled I was in a respectful and evidenced manner.

The Social Media policy is conveniently presented as a pre log-in hurdle which requires the 'logger-on' to tick a single little box to acknowledge that they will never ever, pinkie promise, ever bring the council into 'disrepute'. You have the choice of agree or query. I clicked query and a thirty day countdown began. I chased it up on day twenty-nine and when I asked what happens if I refuse to click 'Agree', I was informed that I would be in breach of my contract! The ambiguous and loose concept is particularly dodgy given that it puts the fear of bejesus into anyone from expressing their feelings and thoughts freely. If you have a family relying on your wage, a mortgage, a gambling debt, hot-tub payments or any financial Albatross around your neck, then the last thing you can afford to do is risk getting sacked. What was that thing called again? You know the one. The thing with the – oh yeah. Article 10 of the Human Rights Act. 'Everyone has the right to freedom of expression. This right shall include freedom to hold opinions and to receive and impart information and ideas without inference by public authority and regardless of frontiers.' Now I am no big city lawyer, but Article 10 highlights how discriminative my employer's social media policy (and that of other local authorities etc) is in relation to our Human Rights.

An alternative progressive and inclusive approach to parenting would act as a herd immunity from stereotypical gender role discrimination.

Rather than reaching for our pitchforks and stirring up

allies to attack 'The Man', surely we are all civilised enough to talk and listen to one another, with respect and integrity for the yearning of a better community for all. Without such discrimination, there will be a hope of creating an ingredient in establishing a better future for those who follow in our footsteps. Resentment is only an anchor that holds us in a stalemate and prevents progress. Humility, clarity, and accountability need to be the order of today in order to ensure that tomorrow and a week next Wednesday, or whenever in the days ahead are more in keeping with the requirements of contemporary family life.

On a more happy-go-lucky glass is full-ish note, in the spirit of hope and positivity I want to take this opportunity to acknowledge and celebrate a timeline of progressive milestones.

Land of milk and honey. Following is the equality story thus far:

(Information sourced from ww.equalityhumanrights.com or otherwise referenced)

1950: The European Convention on Human Rights

An international convention protecting the human rights and political freedoms of the citizens of Europe. Drafted in 1950 by the then newly formed Council of Europe.

1965: Race Relations Act

Introduced because of what the Museum of London described as, 'casual colour prejudice was part of daily life' after the introduction of economic migrants after World War Two. The aim was to outlaw any discrimination on the 'grounds of colour, race, or ethnic or national origins.'

1965: International Convention on the Elimination of All

Forms of Racial Discrimination

This was the first human rights treaty adopted by the United Nations (UN). The International Convention on the Elimination of All Forms of Racial Discrimination (CERD) defines what constitutes race discrimination and sets out a comprehensive framework for ensuring that civil, political, economic and social rights are enjoyed by all, without distinction of race, colour, descent or national or ethnic origin.

1966: UK signs up to the European Court of Human Rights

Six years after the European Court of Human Rights was created, the UK granted what is known as 'individual petition' – the right for people to take their cases directly to the court in Strasbourg.

BONUS FUN FACT.

1974: Sweden

Sweden was the first country to introduce 'Paid Parental Leave' also to fathers in 1974, and this legislation has since then continuously been reformed in order to bring about a more equal parenthood.

(Quoted from Duvander, Ann-Zofie, Ferrarini, Tommy and Sara Thalberg 'Swedish parental leave and gender equality Achievements and reform challenges in a European perspective.')

1975: Sex Discrimination Act

The act made sex discrimination illegal in the areas of employment, education and the provision of goods, facilities and services.

1975: Employment Protection Act.

The UK introduced its first maternity leave legislation.

1976: Race Relations Act

The Race Relations Act was established to prevent race discrimination. It made race discrimination unlawful in employment, training, housing, education and the provision of goods, facilities and services.

1976: International Covenant on Economic, Social and Cultural Rights (ICESCR)

The general principles expressed by the Universal Declaration of Human Rights were given specific legal force through these two covenants. The Universal Declaration of Human Rights, the International Covenant on Civil and Political Rights (ICCPR) and the International Covenant on Economic, Social and Cultural Rights (ICESCR) make up the International Bill of Rights.

1979: Convention on the Elimination of All Forms of Discrimination against Women (CEDAW)

Often referred to as the 'bill of rights for women', the Convention on the Elimination of All Forms of Discrimination against Women defined what constitutes discrimination against women and sets out the core principles to protect their rights.

1984: UN Convention against Torture and Other Cruel, Inhuman or Degrading Treatment or Punishment

The most comprehensive international treaty dealing with torture, the Convention against Torture and Other Cruel, Inhuman or Degrading Treatment or Punishment became the first binding international instrument exclusively dedicated to preventing some of the most serious human rights violations of our time.

1989: UN Convention on the Rights of the Child

Governments worldwide promised all children the same rights by adopting the Convention on the Rights of the Child, also known as the CRC or UNCRC. The basic premise is that children (under the age of 18) are born with the same fundamental freedoms and inherent rights as all human beings, but with specific additional needs because of their vulnerability.

FUN FACT: Let these two specific articles marinate with you (UNICEF.ORG.UK).

Article 3 (Best interests of the child) The best interests of the child must be a top priority in all decisions and actions that affect children.

Article 18 (Parental responsibilities and state assistance) *Both parents* share responsibility for bringing up their child and should always consider what is best for the child. Governments must support parents by creating support services for children and giving parents the help they need to raise their children.

1995: Disability Discrimination Act

This Act represented the first far-reaching legislation on discrimination against disabled people. It covered key areas of life such as employment and training, education, goods, facilities and services, premises and transport.

1998: Human Rights Act

In force since October 2000, the Human Rights Act incorporated into domestic law the rights and liberties enshrined in the European Convention on Human Rights. People in the UK no longer had to take complaints about human rights breaches to the European Court in Strasbourg – British courts could now hear these cases.

FUN FACT: More to marinate upon.

Article 14 of the Human Rights Act 1998 relates to 'Prohibition of discrimination'.

The Act states: 'In the United Kingdom, human rights are protected by the Human Rights Act 1998. Public authorities, like a local authority or the NHS, must follow the Act.

2006: Universal Periodic Review.

The UN's new review system meant that, for the first time, the human rights records of all Member States would come under regular scrutiny through the Universal Periodic Review. It gave a clear message that all countries have scope to improve the way human rights are promoted and protected.

2008: UN Convention on the Rights of Persons with Disabilities (UNCRPD)

The UN Convention on the Rights of Persons with Disabilities (UNCRPD) was the first human rights treaty of the 21st Century. It reaffirms disabled people's human rights and signals a further major step in their journey to becoming full and equal citizens.

2010: the Equality Act.

The Equality Act brought together more than 116 separate pieces of legislation into one single act – a new, streamlined legal framework to protect the rights of individuals and advance equality of opportunity for all.

FUN FACT: As mentioned previously, the Equality Act is the UK citizens' protector of nine specific characteristics. With regards to my story the relevant one being my sex.

This concludes the equalityhumanrights.com timeline.

In addition and more recently:

2015: Shared Parental Leave.

A 'ground-breaking' step towards parental gender equality (on paper). A period of parental leave that can be taken from employment. The inconvenient and discriminative truth being that it stipulates that it exists on a basic statutory pay basis, unlike the more favourable treatment of enhanced pay available for birth mums and adoptive parents. There is a teasing aspect, which states that 'Some employers will offer enhanced pay', dependent on how much they recognise the importance of equality and diversity.

FUN FACT: Also, in this year. The United Nations members (UK featuring heavily) established their Global Goals to make the world a better place by 2030. Global Goal number five being, 'Gender bias is undermining our social fabric and devalues all of us.'

'Adopt and strengthen policies and enforceable legislation for gender equality.'

Two nods to significant recent milestones in UK equality:

2019: National Health Service, Welsh Government, Vodafone, and AVIVA (the latter being very impressive as they are private companies) provide enhanced pay for biological fathers.

Although they were not legally bound to do so, the above recognised their responsibility and accountability in providing enhanced pay for biological dads on par with birth mums and adoptive parents (highlighting how archaic and tokenistic my local authority employers, are.)

2019: For the first time ever all posts in the Armed Forces are open to women and men.

'Women will be allowed to apply for all military roles in the British armed forces, including in frontline infantry units and the Royal Marines, the government has announced.' – Defence Secretary, Gavin Williamson.

Women will also be able to put themselves forward for selection for specialist units including the SAS and SBS. The Ministry of Defence described the move as historic.

An MoD spokesperson said: 'By making all branches and trades of the military open to everyone, regardless of their gender, the armed forces are building on their reputation of being a leading equal opportunities employer.'

All of the aforementioned respondents aka 'culprits' of discrimination are most likely born from uneducated ignorance and unconscious bias. The seed of a culture of equality always begins for every one of us (culprits included) with the attitudes presented by our parents. There is no better representation of the normality of equality than in a family where parental roles are present as an equal partnership. When that is the norm, equality has won, and discrimination has lost.

I have three out of the four oppressive unprotected characteristics that are considered to be fair game to quash at any available opportunity. I am a white, heterosexual man. The only other thing missing that would make an oppressive Royal Flush would be if I was rich. This societally accepted gender bias which appears to be ingrained within a twenty-first century rhetoric as a rite of passage to 'take the power back.'

4
Unconscious Bias

'Concentrate on what you're concentrating on. Don't see the bigger picture. Because if you see the bigger picture, you're gonna say "Why am I even bothering?" I'm a finite life form on a planet with a dying star floating through infinity, trying not to get eaten.'
   Jessimae Peluso – Joe Rogan, #1466.

Unconscious Bias is a posh modern phrase akin to 'ignorance is bliss' in old money. In my family's experience the unconscious bias we experienced related to a blatantly outdated and discriminatory policy. The Shared Parental Leave policy. The policy in fairness does come with 'Some employers do offer enhanced pay' (within the first few paragraphs of my employer's Shared Parental leave policy). Like a baggy dress on an eligible gypsy girl at a dance who is destined to be 'grabbed' by every Tom, Dick, and Harry, the Shared Parental Leave policy teased us mercilessly and continues to do so. The ambiguity and inconsistency is frustrating when compared to the more favourable enhanced pay and provisions within the Maternity Leave and Adoption Leave policies provided by my employers, The Authority.

Even more exasperatingly, I have completely rested on my laurels in my eleven years as an employee at The Authority.

Equality is law, right? Discrimination of all kinds is banished to the realms of the dark, less morally conscious past, right? Wrong. Thanks to good old unconscious bias which continues to prop up the male breadwinner stereotype.

As the number of adoptees in the general population I exist in is in the minority, I am not surprised that the employee populous of The Authority was unaware that an adoptive parent elected as the primary caregiver is entitled to the enhanced pay and provisions as set out in the vastly more well-known Maternity Leave policy. I too was ignorant to this well-deserved and progressive entitlement under the Adoption Leave policy. Therefore, the comparison is likely to never have been made between the marginalisation of biological dads as the poor relations within parental rights at The Authority. Until my wife and I became pregnant.

Here is where the unconscious bias comes in. To paint our picture on a wider 'Great' British landscape, I will ironically borrow from the warm, xenophobic memories of banter with my English brethren (still close friends to this day) during my university days in Stoke-on-Trent circa September 2001. As the sole Welshman in a halls dorm of twelve Englishmen it was banter-rific open season. The lads often mocked my Luddite ways when it came to all things I.T. They had this idea of mid Wales being a backward, hillbilly, banjo playing, inbred land full of farmers and indigenous hill folk. I comfortably laughed off the bants. All four years of it. I always felt proud of my roots and still do to this day. I hope I always will. However, in complete honesty the 'backward' description of attitudes within mid Wales has an accurate sting to it from my recent experience. The lack of progressiveness in the attitudes towards the rights and expectations of fathers from The Authority is undisputed evidence of this.

I have never met a Welshman who has been a stay-at-home dad. At the age of thirty-six I was yet to meet a stay-at-home dad. I am not saying that this is an indictment across the contemporary board of the UK; I am just speaking from my experience within rural mid Wales. If stereotypes are not challenged, nothing will change and the 'ignorance is bliss' attitude of old will repeat generation after generation like a sexist *Groundhog Day*. I am not trying to vilify the whole populous of mid Wales. I get it. If I had not experienced sex discrimination first hand it would not have beeped on my radar and you guessed it. I would be blissfully ignorant too.

I am not the kind of guy to hold a grudge, or so I thought. But, one comment from a keyboard warrior (probably an old-school indigenous hill folk-ian) really grinded my gears. I touched upon this earlier, hence the title of this book. When I raised my disappointment of the lack of parental provisions on the World Wide Web, a person described me as a snowflake. On a forty-five-minute drive between work appointments, my mind ran amok with witty retorts on how best to stick that proverbial in-bred banjo up their arse. Then I realised, I am not James Blunt. People have every right to their opinion. Even if it was in the 0.01% of responses that I received in comparison with the fantastically positive love of the vast majority, it was a reality check for me and it spurred me on even more so to challenge the unconscious, residual ignored bias.

Playing the 'Unconscious Bias Blame Game' is like getting angry at individual rain droplets after an ensuing flood. In my humble opinion, there is far more sustainable benefit in reinforcing flood controls to divert the stereotypical rain drops away from adversity. Such as, challenging the bureaucratic footings of flood barriers.

What is this Unconscious Bias of which I speak? And why is it relevant to my case?

According to www.engageinlearning.com: 'The definition of Unconscious bias revolves around making decisions and judgements quickly which often results in aspects such as gender, race, appearance or other values which are often irrelevant to the decision or judgement being determined.

'Unconscious bias occurs when we need to make decisions and judgements quickly. We draw on our personal experiences. This means there is a natural bias towards views and opinions which fit with the world view we are most familiar and comfortable with. By doing this unconsciously, there is no malicious intent, we are often unaware that we have done it, and of its impact and implications.'

To answer why unconscious bias is relevant to my case, the sentence 'there is a natural bias towards views and opinions which fit with the world view we are most familiar and comfortable with' sums it up perfectly. The current view of the UK and in my case Wales and rural mid Wales in particular, a man is a breadwinner and not a n

Every 2.4 children family, I remember the term 'Nuclear Family', scenario that has been washed over me since day dot has served to create an unconscious bias within myself. Every film, TV show, book, and story I was told included this 'normal' family dynamic. Mummy was the caring and doting housewife and daddy was the patriarchal breadwinning alpha male. Grrrr.

All through my life, this 'normal' has been omnipresent. Primary school teachers, nurses and social workers are predominantly women. Surgeons, prime ministers, doctors, pilots and Armed Forces personnel are predominantly male. All trades-MEN, police-MEN, fire-MEN. That is ingrained within our DNA. Still not sold? Here's a few childhood influences for you. Fireman Sam, Bob the Builder, Super Mario (plumber) and Postman Pat. I am not knocking these legends. All great blokes. Emphasis on blokes.

Growing up, my dad drove a digger and my mum was a dinner lady. All stereotypes for the upcoming generation of the 80s read like men are the providers who get sh*t done, while the dinner ladies fed us, and the Lollipop Ladies helped us to get to where we needed to go. Growing up, my elder brother had a toy farmyard with animals and tractors, a sandpit equipped with toy diggers, toy guns and little Army Men. I played with the ripped, alpha physique action figures which included He-Man, Spiderman, Batman, and Superman. In contrast, my female cousins played with toy kitchens, nurse related toys adorned in female uniform, stethoscope, and first-aid kit, and their figurines were Barbie and Cindy.

Times they are a-changing but said change is barely the tip of the iceberg. My argument reinforces the point that children (particularly us eighties children who are the vast bulk of today's current parent cohort) in our formative years were at our most malleable. If our 2020s babies grow up in a family unit which celebrates equality, partnership, fairness, progressiveness, and diversity, a new moral conscious could be fast-tracked into the status quo.

Some people fear change. All corporations and institutions are change-phobic because their matrix is based on financial budgets. The inclusion of inclusion for dads on par with all other parents will have a front end cost if viewed from a short sighted vantage point. For those forward thinkers, it would be a financial and moral investment in the wellbeing of parents and children. Hence the attempts by my local authority bosses and Employment Tribunal to quash my little, lonely, 'snowflakey' voice.

Furthermore, by the UK government introducing their Shared Parental Leave initiative in 2015, they tried to fob us off with a fugazi. At first glance it appeared to be the real deal. Finally, an impressive and progressive precedent in gender equality within parental roles was established in UK law. But (a very big but) the fact that no enhanced pay was included across the board just undermined the importance of the father's role within the parental unit. Enhanced pay for biological mums and adoptive parents but not for biological dads in my scenario.

What purpose does unconscious bias serve? It reinforces a comfortable, tried and tested (arguably worn out) societal template for families. It appears that (please forgive my generalisation) a successful and age-old model for order within a society is to distract, dumb-down, and control predetermined roles. The Colosseum in ancient Rome is a societal model that springs to mind. Fifty thousand citizens would merge as one within and their collective calendars would be focused on switching off from the norm and turned on to watching Gladiators fight to the death, with one societal common goal. Distraction. And who built the coliseum and arranged the entertainment within? The Senate, that's who. A means of showing love to the citizens. Or, a means by which the Senators subtly distracted the mob from senate business and painted themselves as a power who cared for their underlings. Ring any bells to nowadays? X-Factor, Strictly Come Dancing, Dancing on Ice, I'm a Celebrity, football's

Premier League/International European Cup/World Cups, rugby's Six Nations/World Cup/Autumn Internationals, and the ability to gamble instantly on anything from horse racing to how many corners will be taken in a half of a football match. Case in point, mid Covid-19 lockdown the only institution in our society which is given special treatment was football's premiership. While Welsh people are told to stay home, except for extenuating circumstances such as being a key worker, premier league clubs are back training and getting ready to return to their respective colosseums. Albeit, a physically empty one. However, the online gambling tycoons and streaming/pay-per-view television companies were coiled to backfill the deep hole left in a lot of contemporary lives. In this metaphor, biological dads are a non-league club where the players pay their subs to play and fit football in around their full time jobs. Whereas birth mums and adoptive parents are in the premiership and can get the enhanced pay they deserve to look after their babies. Us dads have a lot of leagues above us and as the current laws state, it will be nigh on impossible to get promoted enough times to reach the premiership with the other parents in my scenario. Unless a Sheikh or Russian tycoon takes over our club that is.

And, arguably the perfect tool for puppeteering the plebs' attitudes and the perfect machine of procrastination, social media. Influencing our thoughts and farming us in furrows of algorithms in a digital field as far as the 'i' can see. The ultimate 'Dot Con' in creating a collective conscious. Or, in this case, a collective unconscious.

According to *Ofcom* (www.ofcom.org.uk):
'Smartphones have become the hub of our daily lives and

are now in the pockets of two thirds (66%) of UK adults, up from 39% in 2012. The vast majority (90%) of 16-24 year olds own one; but 55-64 year olds are also joining the smartphone revolution, with ownership in this age group more than doubling since 2012, from 19% to 50%.

'On average, mobile users spent nearly two hours online each day using a smartphone in March 2015 (1 hour and 54 minutes), compared to just over an hour spent online by laptop and PC users (1 hour and nine minutes).

'But this is still only half of the 3 hours and 40 minutes we spend in front of the TV each day.'

Therefore, if we sleep an average of eight hours a night, we are awake for sixteen hours. Within this awake time (another irony of being zombies rather than awoke), Ofcom states that between TV time and smartphone time, on average we spend nearly five hours and forty minutes of our day using both. That's over a third of our day where we are at the mercy of algorithm marketing, political influence, and societal expectations. Trending, branding, and yearning for likes, shares and love for our personal content. Like the lanes of an enormous motorway, all merging together and signposted to head in the same direction. Final destination, 'On Brand'. Population number, all who dwell within the world of social media. Snowflakes of a biblical snowstorm which inevitably melt and form the same river which carves its way through the landscapes of our communities, societies and world as we know it.

Furthermore, how many of us think it is more important if their football team gets relegated from their league, or if Wales beat England in rugby union, or if Peter Andre wins *I'm A Celebrity*, than parliament passing an act for all employers to provide enhanced pay for all parents, regardless of their gender on parental leave after the birth of a child? Most of society, I imagine.

With regards to my grievance, the fact that as a reasonably on the ball adult, the 2015 Shared Parental Leave policy arrived and left no imprint on my way of life. Not even a ripple. It was not until I was an expectant parent in 2018 that I came across the apparently wonderful and virtuous parental leave option. As mentioned up until this point, parental equality had never even been near my radar, let alone been a blip on it. Prior to this, I had never given it any thought. I had no inkling that there was an option for dads to play a bigger role than that of my dad, or uncles, or brother who all went back to work after their children were born as was the norm. This unconscious bias of parental stereotypes was and still remains a sad indictment of the marginalisation of the rights of the father within the partnership of Planet Parent. We are bred to believe that our place is not in the home with the children and housework but out there, being the alpha and providing for our families. I for one would like to play a role in being 'awoken' to this conditioning by manifesting a glitch in our matrix.

5
Our Story

'The revolution is not an apple that falls when it is ripe. You have to make it fall.' Che Guevara.

This account is our cautionary tale of taking on 'The Man'. In a word, doomed! As it turned out, there was as much chance of us winning our sex discrimination case as there was of me licking my own elbow. To say we had an uphill struggle on our hands is an epic understatement. From the offset, my wife and I, with our first baby in tow, had to make a decision. Drop the whole thing, which we both refused to do, given how strongly we both felt about the discrimination, or punch well above our weight and have a crack at the title.

Our grievance was two pronged. We were told by my employers that I was not eligible to enhanced pay on the Shared Parental Leave policy when birth mums and adoptive parents were. My colleagues of both previously mentioned parental camps shared how ridiculously outdated it was to marginalise biological dads in this way. In addition, my request for Shared Parental Leave took thirteen weeks to process (three weeks prior to our baby's due date) and a future Freedom of Information Request shared that it took birth mums six weeks on average to process their Maternity Leave requests and Adoption Leave requests took three weeks.

Given that we had to juggle first-time parenting at such

short notice and we could not afford to take the statutory pay of the Shared Parental Leave policy, I had to go back to work and reluctantly left my wife in the sole nurturing stereotypical role for our daughter. We agreed that I was best placed to focus on the grievance task at hand. That's right. It was time to get all snowflakey and pursue social justice. In hindsight, it was the most frustrating and draining experience of my thirty-six years on planet Earth. This was down to the abundance of bureaucratic hoops we had to go through. Such as the unconscious bias of parliament, my employers' tokenistic celebration of 'Council Values' such as being progressive, diverse and positive etc, their hypocritical bureaucratic clusterf*ckery stance on their own Equality and Diversity policy, and their seeming arrogance of acting against the Human Rights Act and Equality Act. Evidenced by our own Welsh Government offering enhanced pay for biological mums and dads and adoptive parents and our National Health Service also doing so. My employer's spokespeople shared in reply to articles I shared with local newspapers such as the County Times, Brecon and Radnor Express and even nationally in the Daily Telegraph that they were government bound to offer statutory pay to dads on the Shared Parental Leave policy. Another kick in the family jewels was the Employment Tribunal judge's reluctance to recognise the obvious discrimination I faced. In addition, when I joined the Union in the aftermath of our initial grievance, as an agency they were as useful as a sombrero to a unicorn, because their policy was that they couldn't help as I wasn't a member at the origin of my grievance. Despite a nigh on obsessive prolonged effort, I couldn't get any legal representation or any external agency support to help carry the legal load. Hence, I entered the legal wolves' den in my brand-new sheepskin coat. Doomed to failure!

Despite the previous paragraph of joy, japes and lols, I hope our experience will encourage other regular Joes, Janes and all other chosen identifiable labels to step up and speak up, if and when they feel like they are the victims of social injustice. Despite our literal failure to make the difference we wanted to, I feel so fortunate that I live in a country where I can air my grievance without fear of being silenced by Big Brother (although I occasionally tiptoed this line as you will hear more about later). Even if the legal and employer bureaucratic skulduggery and gamesmanship almost broke me. At the outset, my moral compass was as buoyant as a cork in an armband, fast forward to my day in court sixteen months later and I was as mentally, emotionally, and physically broken as a three-legged snooker table.

I feel so lucky that my wife and I see our relationship as a partnership. We mutually agreed that this campaign had to be followed through to the farthest possible point we could take it, as the issue is ridiculous and bigger than us. We are just nice people, trying to do a nice thing for everyone. We see the benefit of a child being born into an environment of equality where both parents have a partnership and share everything from changing nappies, to washing dishes, to doing the laundry. No additional beef, no hidden agenda, just simply challenging a societal wrong.

Not a Brotherhood versus a Sisterhood. But a universal parenthood. A celebratory flag fluttering aloft on the summit of equality hill for everyone to see. An equality pebble dropped in an ocean whereby outreaching ripples will eventually impact on every aspect of our society. An ethical germination of a universal rhetoric of equality. What a lovely thought.

7
It's OK, we have an Equality and Diversity policy

"What in the hell is diversity?" Champ Kind.
"Well, I could be wrong, but I believe diversity is an old, old wooden ship that was used in the Civil War era." Ron Burgundy.
Channel 4 News Team. Anchorman.

You and I know that Mr Burgundy is way off with his interpretation in the brilliant *Anchorman* (*Anchorman 2*, not so much). Unless somebody called Diversity identified as an old, old wooden ship that was used in the Civil War era, that is. Best I err on the side of caution there.

Initially, way back in the summer of 2018, when I emailed my grievance to Human Resources as to adoptive parents and birth-mums being offered enhanced pay on their respective parental leave provisions when I was not, I felt confident that not only was my moral compass on point, but I also had the understanding that my employers' Equality and Diversity policy would be on point too. A protected characteristic is a protected characteristic. How could there be a different interpretation of that, given that it is based upon the Equality Act (2010) which underpins our way of life and culture within the UK?

Welcome to the whacky and occasionally inept world of local government. I am sure that Billy Smart's Circus had fewer clowns than the management tier of my local authority. To cut away any confusion as to what the Equality and Diversity policy was designed to represent and the purpose of its function, I have the following helpful and clear definitions from the authority of all things 'employee grievance', ACAS (Advisory, Conciliation and Arbitration Service. www.acas.org.uk).

A workplace encouraging equality, diversity and inclusion can help:
- make it more successful
- keep employees happy and motivated
- prevent serious or legal issues arising, such as bullying, harassment and discrimination
- to better serve a diverse range of customers
- improve ideas and problem-solving
- attract and keep good staff

Equality

Equality in the workplace means equal job opportunities and fairness for employees and job applicants.

You must not treat people unfairly because of reasons protected by discrimination law ('protected characteristics'). For example, because of a person's sex, age or race.

'Sex' you say? Hmm. 'Protected Characteristic' you say?

Diversity

Diversity is the range of people in your workforce. For example, this might mean people with different ages, religions, ethnicities, people with disabilities, and both men and women. It also means valuing those differences.

To avoid bullying, harassment or discrimination, you should

make sure:

- your workforce and managers understand what is protected by discrimination law
- what's expected under discrimination law is actually happening in your workplace
- you make changes if what's expected is not happening, for example stepping up staff training
- your workforce and managers understand what the benefits can be of having a range of people with different backgrounds

Inclusion

An inclusive workplace means everyone feels valued at work. It lets all employees feel safe to:

- come up with different ideas
- raise issues and suggestions to managers, knowing this is encouraged
- try doing things differently to how they've been done before, with management approval

An inclusive workplace can help lower the risk of bullying, harassment and discrimination.

My literal understanding, based upon the evidence presented by ACAS, my conclusion is:

1) Staff morale, appreciation and retention benefit from an employer implementing a practical recognition of Equality, Diversity and Inclusion.

2) To quote the band 'Hear'Say', equality rights for employees are 'pure and simple'. Do I have a protected characteristic concerning my grievance? Yes, my sex. Is another sex being treated more favourably than me? Yes, birth-mums. (All other parental types who receive enhanced pay are also treated more favourably as parents).

3) Is what's expected under discrimination law actually

happening in my workplace? No. No, it is not.

4) As an employee do I feel valued and included? No. No, I do not.

To give my grievance some context, after my employers' Human Resources, Pay Roll and Employment Service's conclusion in July 2018, three weeks prior to our first baby's due date, that I was not entitled to enhanced pay on their interpretation of the Shared Parental Leave policy, we shared three concerns. Firstly, we raised:

'I believe that, despite stating that you are committed to the promotion of Equal Opportunities as an employer, the Council is failing to treat female and male employees equally, thereby demonstrating gender discrimination in the workplace. As employers, the Council is legally obliged to offer statutory maternity/paternity pay to both female and male employees, which you do for both maternity/adoptive and shared parental leave schemes. However, by only offering the occupational benefits to female/adoptive employees, the Council is effectively discriminating against male employees who are biological fathers. Please explain why you are doing this?'

Secondly:

'The existing Council policies seem to (inadvertently or not) make gendered assumptions about who is best to deliver childcare for biological parents, to the detriment of your male employees. By not offering male employees the same enhanced occupational benefits as female employees when taking time off to raise the children. The Council's current Shared Paternal Leave pay is prohibiting the shared parental leave being a realistic option for expectant biological fathers to take extended leave unlike expectant mothers. Please can you explain why you cannot simply offer the enhanced benefit of occupational pay to all your employees and why do you feel it is acceptable discriminating against male employees by not offering this benefit to them?'

Thirdly:

'Please can you answer how Powys County Council are being gender equal in offering only female employees and adoptive parents (male or female) occupational maternity/adoption pay, and the statuary maternity/adoption pay, therefore discriminating against male employees who are not offered the same enhanced benefit when taking the shared paternal leave?'

Response from The Authority.

Well, as you have probably worked out by now, the response was not reflective of the council's values or their Equality and Diversity policy with regard to protected characteristics. The gentleman shut the door on our grievance by referring to two cases as a comparison. The cases mentioned were Ali and Hextall. These cases have been an ever-present shadow over part of our grievance until February 2020. The part in respect to our biological factors, and that asks why can't birth mums and biological fathers be offered the same enhanced option of pay so that they can decide as a family with regard to the best way to support their parental responsibilities. The other part being the question as to why an elected adoptive parent is treated more favourably than me, evidenced by the provision of enhanced pay at my workplace.

In order to shine a light on the aforementioned Ali and Hextall cases, here follows a brief summary of both cases:

Ali v Capita Customer Management Ltd.

A father whose wife was advised to return to work to combat post-natal depression has won a sex discrimination claim after his employer told him that he would be paid full pay for only two weeks' paternity leave.

Under the maternity policy, female employees taking maternity leave are entitled to enhanced maternity pay.

Mr Ali argued that the employer's policy assumes that a man caring for his baby is not entitled to the same pay as a woman performing that role, taking away the choice that he and his wife wanted to make for their baby.

According to Mr Ali, this was not a valid assumption to make in 2016.

The employment tribunal upheld Mr Ali's sex discrimination complaint in Ali v Capita Customer Management Ltd. It accepted that men are being encouraged to play a greater role in caring for their babies.

The employment tribunal believed that the role of primary carer is a matter of choice for the parents, but that the choice should be free of "generalised assumptions" that the mother is always best placed to undertake the primary role and should get full pay. (Personnel Today)

A winning decision for Ali at the Employment Tribunal. This was overturned at the Employment Appeal Tribunal on the grounds that, um, well. I have no idea as to why. Just when there looked like there was going to be a common-sensical dawn for equality in parenting, a loud warning shot was fired across their bow which scared the dawn's chorus away.

Hextall v Chief Constable of Leicestershire Police.

A male worker claimed that his employer had discriminated against him because of his sex as he was only entitled to receive statutory shared parental pay, when the employer paid enhanced maternity pay. (Personnel Today)

Hextall lost at the Employment Tribunal and again at the Employment Appeal Tribunal.

On the 28th of May 2019, Rob Moss in Personnel Today reported in 'Employers can enhance maternity pay and not shared parental pay.'

The Court of Appeal has ruled that employers can enhance maternity pay, while only offering statutory shared parental pay for partners.

In two cases that were heard together at the beginning of the month, Ali v Capita and Hextall v Chief Constable of Leicestershire Police, the court said there was "nothing unusual" about their policies and unanimously rejected both claims.

The court did not say when the purpose of maternity leave 'transitioned' into one that focused on caring for the child rather than the mother's health – but indicated this would be at least 14 weeks or longer if the woman was breastfeeding for the recommended six-month period.

While the court's judgment is clear, an increasing number of employers are equalising the parental pay their staff receive. Diversity experts argue that by paying men and women the same when they take leave to look after their children, it can help women share the "motherhood penalty" with fathers.

In the spirit of openness and clarity the following raises why some elements welcomed the Court of Appeal's decision.

Working Families chief executive Jane van Zyl said: "Working Families' intervention in these cases reflects our concern that a ruling of sex discrimination would have undermined the essential protection afforded to women on maternity leave, and could have resulted in employers reducing maternity pay.

"The distinct disadvantage that women face in the workplace having experienced pregnancy and childbirth must continue to be recognised in law. Because maternity leave is designed to protect women's health and wellbeing, it cannot simply be equated with 'childcare'.

"Well-paid leave is vital if we are to improve equality at work and at home, and see more fathers take up their rights. Working Families has long called for employers that can afford to do so to go beyond the minimum pay for shared parental leave, to encourage fathers in particular to use it.

"In addition, we continue to advocate for a properly paid, standalone period of extended paternity leave for fathers. These steps would allow fathers be more involved in their children's lives and help challenge gendered ideas around who works and who cares. Measures like these should complement, not threaten, the rights of working mothers."

Ali and Hextall were not satisfied with this outcome and appealed to the highest court in our lands, The Supreme Court. The flame of hope remained…

Until February 18th, 2020.

'A highly anticipated case to test whether it is discriminatory for employers to enhance maternity pay while not doing the same for shared parental pay has been refused permission to appeal at the Supreme Court.' Rob Moss – Personnel Today.

In short, a shambles. This would not only have been a win for dads, but a win for mums too. Instead, the same tired old trodden paths are to be trodden yet again, where more law firms will cash in on the creaky and archaic justice system, until a date in five, ten, or fifteen years' time when the system will catch up with contemporary needs. Another example of the tokenism of the Human Rights Act and the Equality Act.

One final thought to leave with you. My wife and I were so invested in the journey of these cases that we sat through a live feed of the Court of Appeal's deliberations of the cases back in May 2019. One of the judges stated (not verbatim as I'm paraphrasing from memory here) with regards to dads receiving enhanced pay on Shared Parental Leave, 'It is not a fair comparator because a dad could get a second job during shared parental leave.' My wife and I suddenly realised that we were a long, long, way from Kansas. If I suggested a mother could get a second job while on maternity leave, I would have been shot down and vilified as a misogynist. That was the moment we realised that our vision of common sense, equality and parental equality was as likely as a bull lactating.

Back to the grievance response.

We were disappointed with the transparency of the response. Firstly, the cases of Hextall and Ali, they were still live and obvious to anyone with as much knowhow as he clearly had, that they were contentious issues which could be appealed. As a lay person I could have just taken his word for this, had I not followed it up. In our opinion, there was an absence of clarity and transparency regarding this. If he had added, 'these cases are still live and in the spirit of clarity I suggest you contact Citizens' Advice or seek legal advice', council values would have been present.

Secondly, no closure was offered to explain why Adoption Leave follows the same provisions as set out in the Maternity Leave policy, when Shared Parental Leave does not. If he had shared that, 'if you are still unsatisfied, you can contact ACAS whose role is to address such grievances', we could have felt like we had been treated with openness and respect.

We considered the response to our complaint by the Professional Lead of Human Resources and Development to be confusing and misleading, it lacked clarity and was very final. There is no mention in his email of an appeal option, or a suggestion of approaching UNISON if we were unhappy with his response. Or any offer of a face-to-face meeting to ensure there was absolute clarity in order to find closure. In my opinion, the latter being the crux of a lot of my employers' problems. A good old-fashioned 'sit down' and respectful discussion over a cuppa and a biscuit. The human touch. A touch of mutual respect. The lost touch of diplomacy some would say. From my experience in general, the farther up the totem pole of hierarchy, the more detached and colder the individuals tend to become.

Just a reminder and to 'touch base' moving forward on our corporate journey together. The published Council Values at the time of our grievance in 2018 were 'Positive, Progressive, Professional, Open and Collaborative'. Sounds clear and very straightforward. Our response was far from progressive, open or collaborative.

For clarity, here is the current corporate narrative, which has since piggy-backed onto the Council Values. Readers, let me introduce you to 'Vision 2025.'

Vision 2025 is the council's long term vision which sets out its top priorities and key milestones.

The Corporate Improvement Plan is the road map to Vision 2025. It looks at the next steps that will need to be taken to meet the priorities, and the improvements people can expect to see when the plan is delivered. The plan provides an important framework for engaging residents, councillors, staff and other stakeholders in the council's vision and priorities.

The aim is to create a council of the future that is driven by the right culture and behaviours, delivering high performance and value for money for our communities.

My favourite aim is the creation of a council of the future driven by the 'right culture' and 'behaviours'. One of 'high performance' and exercising value for money for our communities.

The Equality and Diversity policy and the values of which I speak.

The following policies were relevant at the time of the origin of our challenge in 2018.

CYNGOR SIR POWYS COUNTY COUNCIL Grievance Policy and Procedure.

'7.1 (Page 6) The Council is determined to create a public service for the future that is **driven by the right culture and behaviours**. Further to this, the Council wants to deliver high performance and value for our communities.

'7.2 (Page 7) **Values are important to the Council** and therefore wants its culture and working environment to reflect this.'

I am hopeful that my claim highlights the respondent's lack of determination and drive to establish a culture that is 'right'. From our experience the importance of said values are tokenistic and the working environment I am experiencing reflects a culture of inequality where I am being marginalised as a biological father.

CYNGOR SIR POWYS COUNTY COUNCIL Equality and Diversity Policy Statement.

'1.1 (Page 3) Powys County Council (hereinafter "the

Council") is fully committed to removing discrimination and advancing equality of opportunity within the employment of our staff and in the provision of services to our clients and customers, by treating people according to their needs. The Council recognises that our employment and services must be accessible to and appropriate for different types of people, and it is therefore fully committed to providing fully accessible employment provision and services.'

Clearly the highlighted claims in 1.1 raises that I have not been treated with 'equality and diversity' as there is a blatant failure in removing discrimination (based upon the lack of provision of enhanced pay, the incredibly long thirteen week Shared Parental Leave process of administration, and the lack of parents taking up Shared Parental Leave). Rather than 'advancing equality of opportunity' the respondents have actually acted on the contrary and restricted the opportunity for me to achieve equality. Most damningly regarding 'treating people according to their needs', the respondents cannot evidence that they have recognised my needs, let alone treated me according to my needs. This is proven by the respondents exacerbating the stress and development of anxiety for myself, my expectant wife and close family due to leaving us in the lurch as to what I would be entitled to regarding financial support until three weeks before the due date of our first child.

'1.3 (Page 3) The Council recognises that people's differences can mean that some individuals face discrimination or harassment in everyday life and that it therefore has a responsibility to ensure that this is removed in the employment that it provides and in the provision of services to the public.'

In 1.3 the respondent has completely failed in its

responsibility to ensure that 'discrimination in everyday life is removed'. This is proven by the fact enhanced pay was not offered to me as a father on Shared Parental Leave and the puzzling reasons behind why it took thirteen weeks for me to receive my Shared Parental Leave confirmation. Surely, the professional individuals involved in the process of my request can't be so collectively inefficient resulting in a thirteen-week ordeal, when Maternity Leave requests took six weeks and Adoption Leave take three weeks on average respectively.

There has been a lack of efficiency to process my Shared Parental Leave request. This shows that because I was the first employee at Powys County Council to request the Shared Parental Leave in 2018, (since its implementation in 2015) there is a systemic failure within the culture of Powys County Council in recognising its responsibility to promote the options available and to provide equality and diversity for male employees (whose only avenues to co-parent were the less favourable options via Shared Parental Leave and Additional Paternity/Partner Leave). The Freedom of Information request regarding Shared Parental Leave shared that there have only been two employees who have taken up the Shared Parental Leave option up until 2018. Both males.

The Shared Parental Leave and Additional Paternity/Partner Leave fail to provide equality for fathers because of its refusal to offer enhanced pay. The thirteen-week delay in our case highlighted an innate lack of an institutional commitment to recognise and implement the Shared Parental Leave, disenfranchising fathers by alienation via policy.

'1.4 (page 3) The Council is fully committed to complying with the Equality Act 2010 concerning unfair discrimination, advancing equality of opportunity and the promotion of good relationships between different types of people both in the workplace and in the interaction of providing services to the public.'

The statement that 'The Council is fully committed to complying with the Equality Act 2010' is highly ironic in my case. I have yet to experience any commitment to equality regarding my gender, or my role as a biological father in our case.

2. Responsibility

'2.1. Whilst the implementation of this Policy is the responsibility of each and every employee, day-to-day implementation of it will rest with the Heads of Service, under the strategic guidance of the senior Management Team of the Council – the Chief Executive and Directors. Ultimate responsibility will however rest upon the Cabinet in particular and progressed forward by the Cabinet member with the portfolio responsibility for Equality. Appropriate training, development and awareness-raising events will be provided to employees and Members as appropriate.'

The 'responsibility' clearly falls upon the heads of service, senior management team, chief executive and directors to establish and implement acceptable values. These are currently lacking for biological fathers within the cultural institution of Powys County Council.

Rather than being a drowned out little voice in a cacophony of equality protesters. The silence is deafening. This renders the values, visions, policies, and acts utterly tokenistic, hypocritical, and redundant. In the Premiership of Protected Characteristic, Team Dad's Rights United are propping up the table. All the other teams are packing out their stadium's week in, week out. Team Dad's Rights United (TDR

United) are reliant on a few staunch regular season-ticket holders. We are doomed to remain anchored at the bottom of the table until we get a few class grassroots players who catch the attention of the rest of the teams and their respective supporters. If LGBTQ Rovers or Christian City Albion were being marginalised, like TDR United, there would be an uproar. There would be Twitter trending, marches, celebs would be tripping over one another to hashtag their support for change. Politicians' ears would prick up and they would be clambering upon the social injustice bandwagon, faster than they can say 'Look, look. I'm relevant. Vote for me!' Well, at least we cannot get relegated. Or can we?

It could be argued that, as men have stood at the helm of HMS Patriarchy Privilege for so long, it is time for us to pay some reparation to the other groups who have been downtrodden throughout history. An attitude which ironically fails to address equality within the contemporary parental partnership.

8
The Hunt for Support: Take 1

"Inside every cynical person, there is a disappointed idealist."
   George Carlin.

In the rugged spirit of Tommy Lee Jones' character in *The Fugitive*, I left no stone unturned in my hunt for support. I needed someone, anyone, to listen up. My employers had been on the run for thirteen weeks. Average foot speed over uneven policies barring the broken moral compass of four managers and their assistants was snail pace. That gave us a radius of unsurmountable procrastination. What I wanted from each and every one of any potential saviours was a hard target search of common sense and equality from every golf course, office space, councillor chambers, warehouse, farmhouse, hen house, outhouse, and doghouse in the county. The fugitive's name was Powys County Council. Go get them!

   First up, my wife and I wanted an independent person we trusted to run their eye over the response. Mainly because we were too close to the grievance and too emotive. A friend of mine suggested his dad, who is also a friend of mine I should add, as he is a Human Rights lecturer. His name is Sam. He kindly agreed to check it out and fed back with the following:

   'I have looked at the PCC's Supporting Working Parents Policy: A Guide to Maternity, Paternity and Adoption Entitlements and it would appear to provide the basis for you to obtain leave on the rate of pay that applies to maternity leave. This is based on its provisions in relation to adoption constituting an appropriate comparator for you.

'The key point here is that the EAT decision in Mr M Ali v Capita Customer Management does not apply in respect of an adoptive parent. This case stated that the purpose of maternity leave for a woman who has given birth is her health and well-being following pregnancy, confinement and childbirth. It is not based on the care of the child. Quite simply, this does not apply in relation to the adoption of a child. The entitlement of adoptive parents, therefore, is based on the care provisions of the child. As a result, it is appropriate for you to claim the same entitlement as indicated within my employer's Supporting Working Parents Policy at the time of our grievance.'

Thanks to the kindness and nous of Sam, it was 'Go Time!' We needed a savvy voice, an impartial advocate and someone with the clout to make a Local Authority stand up and listen. The 'Hunt for Support - Take 1' led us to the Advisory, Conciliation and Arbitration Service, better known as ACAS. Our tails were up and confidence was high. I called ACAS, completed an online application and was soon allocated a conciliator July 30th 2018. Bear in mind, our first baby was due on August 9th 2018. Therefore, we were extremely grateful that we could pass our grievance to a professional while we focused on the birth of our baby. Things were looking up.

August the 9th came and went and on August 13th we were blessed with our perfect and healthy daughter Eliza. We were first time parents and grateful to have a fortnight where I was fortunate enough to have paternity leave. Hanging over us was the unfortunate reality of us needing to scramble around for childcare from family and friends when I returned to work.

The 16th of August came around, Eliza was three days old. Our conciliator was lovely. She was professional, progressive, positive, open and collaborative. I have heard those values before somewhere! Our conciliator's email was as follows:

'I have now established contact with the Council, due to staff leave I have not yet had a meaningful discussion with them – I anticipate this will take place next week, and look forward to updating you at that time.

'Given that your Early Conciliation deadline is 26th August and I will be unable to get any meaningful discussion underway until week commencing 20th August, it may be worthwhile considering an extension to your deadline. I am able to extend a deadline by a one-off period of 14 days where both parties approve it, and where I can see there is a reasonable prospect of us reaching a resolution in the extended period.'

We were grateful to our conciliator for her efforts and requested an extension in the hope of a satisfactory outcome. A friend and colleague persistently shared a mantra with me whenever this conversation point came up: 'Bazza. It's so predictable. The council will just delay, deny, defend.' This prophecy was as accurate as the 'Talking Clock.' (If this is an unfamiliar thing to you, back in the day of village payphones when we used to dial 123 to see how long we had left before we had to get home for teatime. Simpler times.)

Roll on to August 31st:

'There is still scope for us to explore a resolution. As your certificate was issued to you on 27th August you have been free to lodge a claim from that date; as long as your original approach to ACAS was on time, you have at least one calendar month from the date on the certificate in order to do so. During this interim period, we can continue to explore a resolution, and I anticipate speaking with the Council next week to that end'. (Our conciliator)

I replied on September 3rd, 2018 with:

'That's great thank you. Given that I have until September 27th to lodge a claim **(to the Employment Tribunal)** I will wait until after next week (from Monday 18th September) so that Powys have ample time to discuss a potential resolution with you on our behalf.

'One more thing please. Where do I send our claim? Is there a particular tribunal referral pathway?'

This email sums up my cluelessness and the lack of proactivity of my employers. On the 4th of October I emailed our conciliator with:

'Have you got an update from Powys' perspective please? I'm hoping common sense will prevail on their behalf and there will be amendments made instead of a Tribunal Hearing.

'I have a Tribunal Hearing date set for January 14th.'

Unfortunately, over the period of the 16th of August to the 4th of October 2018, our ACAS conciliator was unable to have a meaningful discussion with our employers, let alone contemplate any sort of resolution. ACAS Conciliator, was unable to have a meaningful discussion with my employers, let alone contemplate any sort of resolution. The process was akin to someone helpful knocking on someone's door for thirty-six working days (or forty-nine days in total if I was to sell the point assertively) and occasionally a few words came out from the door when it was occasionally ajar.

Is anyone thinking 'delay, deny, defend' by any chance?

9
Societal Benefits of Parental Equality

"If you don't like what's being said, change the conversation."
Don Draper. Mad Men.

So, it was around this time in our lives, and 'on our journey moving forward', that it was time to pipe down or roll the dice. By making an application to the Employment Tribunal and receiving confirmation that I would need to be prepared and ideally represented by a professional for our Employment Tribunal Hearing on January 14th 2019, we had rolled the dice!

We were genuinely aghast that we were heading down this path as the common sense plan, in our humble opinions, would have been for there to have been a face-to-face conciliation facilitated by ACAS, between my family and my employers. Something that would not only have been in keeping with their council values, but it would also have saved them thousands of pounds on paying for the service of a barrister to defend them at an Employment Tribunal Hearing. I wondered, and still wonder, why the council has a salaried legal department if they are unable to mediate and potentially divert grievances away from legal proceedings OR (a big or) represent the council at Employment Tribunals. A wondering I have not followed up as methinks I have poked the bear enough already.

Nonetheless, if we wanted to pursue our grievance we had no other formal path to take. We had bought our ticket and were heading to the David versus Goliath showdown in three months' time. Time to get our heads around the whys and whats of all that was the marginalisation of biological dads' rights.

It was around this time when we were running around like headless chickens trying to keep all of our plates spinning, when my wife and I had a crisis talk. As I had to go back to work and the lion's share of the parental and home life responsibilities fell to the lioness. A reality that gave us all the more drive to pursue our grievance and encourage more folks to talk about it. Given our reality, we decided that this grievance would be my responsibility as to avoid any unnecessary stress falling on my wife Laura. We drew a line in the sand and I was flying solo for the foreseeable.

Bearing in mind that I lived and worked in Wales, my first port of call were the Welsh Government. What was their take on all this tomfoolery? Here is what I found out and later used as part of my evidence for my Employment Tribunal Hearing. Fortunately for us, or so I naively thought, the Welsh Assembly Government had shared their findings of 'Work it out: parenting and employment in Wales', three months prior on the 16th of July 2018. It found the following:

We are also excited by the work and developments that the Welsh Government have began as a result of the findings of their comprehensive 'Work it Out: Parenting and Employment in Wales, July 2018.' The report highlighted Flexible working, childcare, and culture change is needed in Wales to achieve gender equality at work. The report states gender inequality is not a new phenomenon, and Wales needs bold action to deliver real and lasting change. The report quotes on p28 "Fair work" should mean equal workplaces, where people have opportunities to progress in their careers while managing their caring responsibilities, without discrimination.

While employment law is not devolved, the Welsh Government still has a key role in eradicating discrimination by modernising workplaces and strengthening the obligations on public bodies, and private and voluntary organisations that receive public funding.

Page 12 states - "While legislation and regulation are important to protect women from pregnancy and maternity discrimination, sustainable change will only be achieved if we are able to shift culture and attitudes so that care is no longer seen as a women's issue and our workplace structures enable parents to effectively balance work and care."

Page 16 states - "By 2030, one in five UK workers will be a mother. Without significant changes to workplace structures, gendered assumptions about childcare, and the eradication of discrimination, mothers will continue to be more likely to be trapped in part-time, low-paid work with fewer opportunities for career progression. This is a key cause of gender inequality, and represents a loss to the economy."

By only offering the statutory pay to employees taking shared parental leave Powys County Council are continuing to make gendered assumptions about childcare provision for their employees. By not providing fathers the opportunity to take up the leave due to the discriminatory difference in pay biological fathers are treated less favourably than their parental counterparts. (In our specific case, we are treated less favourably than adoptive parents at Powys County Council too).

The Welsh Government report on page 48 also found from talking to witnesses that - "Many suggested that improving take up could help challenge gender stereotypes and help reduce pregnancy and maternity discrimination. Maternity Action told us that current arrangements are complex. This, combined with low shared parental leave pay, as well as the attitude and culture of employers, mean take up is very low. 98 In Wales, only 250 fathers benefited from shared parental leave in 2016-17."

Chwarae Teg suggested that the Welsh Government and local authorities should publish employees' take up of shared parental leave. This is relevant as it shows that individual local authorities are responsible for promoting and establishing a Shared Parental Leave policy that is fit for purpose, clear and challenges gender bias.

The report goes on to state on page - "Working to improve access to shared parental leave could contribute to changing cultural attitudes towards women in work. If employers considered that there was an equal chance of a man taking parental leave as a woman, ingrained gendered assumptions could be undone."

UNISON noted that "whilst a legal framework to allow shared parental leave is now available, men feel culturally unable and unwilling to apply, leading to increased pressure on women to shoulder the responsibility".

It was recommended that "the Welsh Government should use all levers of influence to improve the take-up, through business advice, the Economic Contract and by encouraging other public sector bodies and third sector organisations to do the same."

The cultural injustice of the Gender Pay Gap will not change until fundamental rights of parenting, such as enhanced pay for all parents who choose to take primary care for their baby changes. The current lack of diversity, gender equality and inclusivity is glaringly apparent within Powys County Council. The findings of Work it out: parenting and employment in Wales (16/07/2018) that are relevant to this case are as follows -

Inflexible workplace structures, gendered assumptions about

childcare, and wide-scale discrimination mean mothers are more likely to be trapped in part-time, low-paid work with fewer opportunities for career progression. (According to the National Assembly committee)

"During the course of our inquiry we heard some shocking individual experiences: women who lost their jobs during maternity leave, careers derailed because of the lack of flexible work, and fathers prevented from taking on caring responsibilities because of cultural attitudes," said John Griffiths AM, Chair of the Equality, Local Government and Communities Committee.

A series of recommendations were made. The most relevant were 'Recommendation 8. We recommend that the Welsh Government commits to eradicating pregnancy and maternity discrimination in the foundation and thematic sectors as a priority. To monitor this, employees of businesses in receipt of Government support should be surveyed on issues such as discrimination and unfair treatment.'

Recommendation 10. We recommend that the Welsh Government requires third sector organisations accessing financial support to offer flexible working, demonstrate action to reduce gender pay gaps and to report on maternity retention rates, by including these as key criteria in funding contracts.

Recommendation 11. We recommend that the Welsh Government requires businesses to provide flexible working, demonstrate action to reduce gender pay gaps, and report on maternity retention rates as part of procurement arrangements.

Recommendation 12. We recommend that the Welsh Government includes a distinct gender element in the definition of "fair work". The definition used by the Economic Contract should ensure that public funding is only provided to organisations that adhere to equal opportunities and workplace structures that allow women and men to progress in their careers.

After reading this I felt even more confident that there is substance to our grievance which does not just affect me in a silo. It affects all parents in Wales, as the WAG's findings point out. Given these findings it is likely to be the case in the rest of the United Kingdom too. The shackles of parental provision were utterly taut and I felt so confidently that people in my boat who were willing to complain would be that extra pressure required to bust those chains and unshackle this archaic and institutionalised attitude towards parental provisions.

Now that I was confident of the issues raised in Wales it was time to bolster my argument by broadening my horizons to the rest of the United Kingdom and beyond. Next stop, *MenCare*.

They share that: 'MenCare is a global fatherhood campaign active in more than 50 countries on five continents, coordinated by Promundo and Sonke Gender Justice. Our mission is to promote men's involvement as equitable, nonviolent fathers and caregivers in order to achieve family well-being, gender equality, and better health for mothers, fathers, and children. We aim for men to be allies in supporting women's social and economic equality, in part by taking on more responsibility for childcare and domestic work. We believe that true equality will only be reached when men are taking on 50 percent of the world's child care and domestic work.' (https://men-care.org/)

I had never heard of this initiative prior to finding myself in our parental predicament. Here was some more vindication of the wrongs we needed to at the very least try and put right. MenCare published, 'HELPING DADS CARE New U.S. National Survey Confirms Societal Expectations, Limited

Paternity Leave and Insufficient Support Keep Fathers from Taking Leave.'

IN SUMMARY: WHAT WE NEED TO SUPPORT FATHERS

Our survey confirms that men want to be involved caregivers. What holds them back are outdated societal expectations and whether they receive the support they need from their workplace, as well as other social touchpoints. By supporting fathers, we can enable them to be the best they can be at work and at home. In turn, paternity leave would help contribute to improving gender equality in society, further empowering women to be their best across the different domains in their lives. By supporting fathers, employers can improve their recruitment and retention of top talent: both men who might leave to be fully involved at home and women who can find the time to excel at work when their male partners are fully involved with child care.

TO HELP FATHERS BE ALL THEY WANT TO BE, AND FOSTER A MORE EQUITABLE SOCIETY, WE NEED:

GREATER AVAILABILITY TO SUBSTANTIVE, PAID PARENTAL LEAVE, FOR BOTH MEN AND WOMEN, SUPPORTED BY LEGISLATION AND/OR SUPPORTIVE CORPORATE POLICES.

WORKPLACES TO OFFER FLEXIBLE WORKING ARRANGEMENTS, ACTIVELY ENCOURAGE MEN AND WOMEN TO TAKE ADVANTAGE OF SUCH POLICIES, AND COMMUNICATE THEY WILL NOT BE PENALIZED WHEN THEY TAKE PARENTAL LEAVE.

CHANGES IN SOCIETAL EXPECTATIONS: WE NEED TO SHOWCASE EXAMPLES OF FATHERS CARING FOR THEIR CHILDREN TO HELP CATALYZE NEW SOCIAL NORMS.

CELEBRATE MOTHER'S AND FATHER'S CAREGIVING, AND THEIR ROLES IN THE LIVES OF THEIR CHILDREN.

As you can probably imagine, by this point I was nigh on convinced of romping home with a victory at the upcoming Employment Tribunal. I then knew what Frankie Dettori felt like as he galloped home towards the finishing line at the Grand National with all other competitors trailing in his wake. The benefits obviously benefit children, parents, and society as a whole.

In case you are still unconvinced, here is a summary from the Netflix 'Explained' documentary 'Why Women Are Paid Less.'

When making a comparison of men and women the documentary initially focused on Childcare and housework commitments. When comparing working mums and working dads, PEW Research Centre 2013 found in their study *'Number of Hours Spent Each Week On Child Care Or Household Activities'*, that mums spent twenty-five hours in comparison with dads who spent sixteen hours undertaking them. That is nine hours per week extra. Over a year that's the equivalent to an extra three months of a full time job.

This is the nucleus of what's wrong in the parental partnership. Stripped bare, there isn't a partnership (on the whole). When children are raised with this message, stereotypes are formed, normed, and reciprocally performed. Thus, the stereotypical imbalance lives on.

When a baby arrives, the trajectory spikes as our predisposed family norm values are reinforced. The journey of far less resistance is that of the 'nurturing' parent to take the lion's share of parental and care activities, whilst the 'breadwinning cavemen' take the path of least resistance, remaining in work. Therefore, which parent is the most likely to get a work promotion? The little lady, who is at home taking a career break to nurture? Or the big swinging Poppa Bear who is still in the workplace? This divergence continues after maternity leave as most mums work part-time or more flexibly. Whereas dads can continue to be a consistent working presence on a full-time basis and inevitably reap the rewards of their reliability.

The Danish study *'CHILDREN AND GENDER INEQUALITY: EVIDENCE FROM DENMARK*. Henrik Kleven. Camille Landais. Jakob Egholt Sogaard. January 2018 shared that:

Mum's pay trajectory plummets just prior to their child's birth, increases slightly after a year and maintains that level for the next eight years. In comparison, a dad's pay trajectory generally remains unaffected by their child's birth. This study also shows how this pay gap is relevant between a woman with kids and a woman without kids. Therefore, it is not purely a Man v Woman scenario. It is an institutional failing whereby mums have a predisposed pay imbalance because of societal expectations. Women with children versus everyone else. Also known as a 'Motherhood Penalty.' A counter argument being the question around value. A mum who chooses to be a primary carer may believe that true wealth is nurturing and raising their baby as opposed to materialistic monetary value. A pay gap based on choices. A choice that is fraught with financial reliability on the father's financial clout.

If my tail wasn't up before I Netflix and chilled, it most certainly was now. This was going to be so blatantly straightforward. This whole social injustice campaigning malarkey was a walk in the park.

As things stood and still stand, if daddy continues to bring home the bacon, mum can choose to cook and eat the bacon with the family. I feel that it is also worth recognising that the traditional nuclear family of a mum, dad, and 2.4 children are no longer the only recognised and valued societal family blueprint, such as single parents, same sex parents. or parents who identify themselves in a completely different way. I understood that these deeply rooted issues of stereotypes were not going to change overnight. Pardon the pun, it was going to require baby steps. Baby steps.

The responsibility for said steps lies firmly at the fingertips of the bureaucratic behemoth. It does not take a rocket scientist to work out that ensuring parity for all parents who take shared leave with enhanced pay will ignite a spark in a lift-off towards equality. By making businesses accountable to adhere to their Equality and Diversity policies and values; by incentivising small businesses and the self-employed to support parental leave, and by the legal institutions setting progressive precedents, we will be engineering a future of parental equality for the generations that follow.

Whenever we drop the ball in the UK I have a habit of turning my attention to our Scandinavian cousins. With regards to parental equality, Sweden, Finland, and Iceland tend to be at the positive and progressive forefront of righteous change.

As previously mentioned, in 1974, Sweden introduced non-gender specific parental leave. A year before the UK introduced the Maternity Leave policy. Iceland introduced obligatory parental leave for dads since 2000. A use it or lose it scenario. Regarding Finland, according to an article in The Guardian by Alexandra Topping, February 11th, 2020:

'Under new rules, all Finnish mothers and fathers will both get nearly seven months' paid leave, half of which will be non-transferable, while all references to maternity and paternity leave are being scrapped. That sends a very clear message: all parents, from all types of families, are equal in this endeavour.

Compare this to the UK, where much-trumpeted shared parental leave was first introduced five years ago. Only around three in seven families are eligible (agency workers and those on zero hours contracts are excluded), and of those only about 1% have shared any leave at all. By any reckoning it is, according to Adrienne Burgess of the Fatherhood Institute, "an inequitable and failed policy".

Following on from Adrienne Burgess's acutely accurate statement it seems obvious that the UK in 2020 persists in failing to reinforce positive Scandinavian-esque cultural readjustments. Charity begins at home, love begins at home, equality begins at home. Home is the catalyst for hope.

The most frustratingly intrinsic bullshit of my grievance, is that there seems to be a misconception that I am after my pound of flesh as a matter of male principle. Some kind of snowflake vendetta against the female population. This could not be farther from the true desire of what I am trying to do. The societal benefits to families and forming an investment in our children's perception of equality could literally make our world a better place. Full stop.

To prove my point even farther, let's check out the views of a leading sociologist Michael Kimmel, in his Ted Talk. 'Why Gender Equality Is Good For Everyone – Men Included.' May 2015. According to his Ted Talk bio:

'Michael Kimmel is among the leading researchers and writers on men and masculinity in the world. He is the executive director of the Center for the Study of Men and Masculinities at Stony Brook University, where he is also Distinguished University Professor of Sociology and Gender Studies.'

In a nutshell, this guy knows his shit. His Ted Talk summarises:

- Gender equality is good for countries. It turns out, according to most studies, that those countries that are the most gender equal are also the countries that score highest on the happiness scale.
- It is also good for companies. Research by Catalyst and others has shown conclusively that the more gender-equal companies are, the better it is for workers, the happier their labor force is. They have lower job turnover. They have lower levels of attrition. They have an easier time recruiting. They have higher rates of retention, higher job satisfaction, higher rates of productivity. So the question I'm often asked in companies is, "Boy, this gender equality thing, that's really going to be expensive, huh?" And I say, "Oh no, in fact, what you have to start calculating is how much gender inequality is already costing you. It is extremely expensive." So it is good for business.
- And the other thing is, it's good for men. It is good for the kind of lives we want to live, because young men especially have changed enormously, and they want to have lives that are animated by terrific relationships with their children. They expect their partners, their spouses, their wives, to work outside the home and be just as committed to their careers as they are.

- Younger men today expect to be able to balance work and family. They want to be dual-career, dual-carer couples. They want to be able to balance work and family with their partners. They want to be involved fathers.
- Now, it turns out that the more egalitarian our relationships, the happier both partners are. Data from psychologists and sociologists are quite persuasive here. I think we have the persuasive

numbers, the data, to prove to men that gender equality is not a zero-sum game, but a win-win. Here's what the data show. Now, when men begin the process of engaging with balancing work and family, we often have two phrases that we use to describe what we do. We pitch in and we help out.

- When men share housework and childcare, their children do better in school. Their children have lower rates of absenteeism, higher rates of achievement. They are less likely to be diagnosed with ADHD. They are less likely to see a child psychiatrist. They are less likely to be put on medication.

- When men share housework and childcare, their wives are happier. Duh. Not only that, their wives are healthier. Their wives are less likely to see a therapist, less likely to be diagnosed with depression, less likely to be put on medication, more likely to go to the gym, report higher levels of marital satisfaction. So when men share housework and childcare, their wives are happier and healthier, and men certainly want this as well. When men share housework and childcare, the men are healthier. They smoke less, drink less, take recreational drugs less often. They are less likely to go to the ER but more like to go to a doctor for routine screenings. They are less likely to see a therapist, less likely to be diagnosed with depression, less likely to be taking prescription medication. So when men share housework and childcare, the men are happier and healthier. And who wouldn't want that?

- So, what we found is something really important, that gender equality is in the interest of countries, of companies, and of men, and their children and their partners, that gender equality is not a zero-sum game. It's not a win-lose. It is a win-win for everyone. And what we also know is we cannot fully empower women and girls unless we engage boys and men. We know this. And my position is that men need the very things that women have identified that they need to live the lives they say they want to live in order to live the lives that we say we want to live.

Is there really anything else to say. If you are still not convinced, how about analysing things from a psychological perspective. Here follows a study regarding the unappreciated importance of dads as attachment figures.

Counselling Today (ct.counselling.org)

Viewing fathers as attachment figures. By Ashley Cosentino. September 5, 2017.

The role of fatherhood has changed over the years. Hundreds of years ago, the father was the most important parent for raising the children, then he became the breadwinner, and today an expansive volume of research details a general lack of involvement by fathers in their children's lives. Plenty of fathers want to be a part of their children's lives and do whatever they can to stay involved. However, many fathers encounter barriers created by myths that limit, or in some cases prevent, their ability to engage with their children.

Many people may believe some common myths about fathers. These myths include:

Fathers are not interested in being involved.

Fathers do not have the capability to be involved.

Fathers are harmful if they are involved.

There is little to no effect if a father is not involved (or, relatedly, the hassle of dealing with the father is worse than any negative effects that his lack of involvement might have on children).

In reality, both fathers and mothers are important, and not just as a means of feeding, bathing and sheltering their children. Their importance extends beyond meeting the family's physical and safety needs.

John Bowlby established attachment theory in the 1950s and 1960s as an addition to psychoanalytic theory. Attachment theory is a secure base from which to explore close relationships that can accommodate an extensive variability of methods and findings. Attachment theory proposes that affectional bonds are essential to the survival of humans.

Bowlby's original construction of attachment theory proposed the role of the father as ambiguous, but he later recognized that fathers are imperative as attachment figures. Bowlby's philosophy about the role of fathers as attachment figures developed over time with the publication of applicable research findings.

The infant-father attachment turned out to be prevalent while Bowlby was working on his second, more clearly defined version of attachment theory, published in 1969. He found that the father's reactions to the child form the pattern of the child-father attachment relationship. Bowlby's son, Richard Bowlby, who has also lectured and written on attachment theory, has said that he suspects his father's initial concentrated focus on mothers and their attachment role may have ended up prejudicing subsequent research and distorting cultural values.

Bowlby added fathers as significant attachment figures because two distinct attachment roles seemed to exist for two separate but equally important functions for a child's development. One attachment role is to deliver love and security, and the other role is to participate in exciting and challenging practices. In other words, the bond of attachment is more than keeping children safe from danger, which is often seen as the mother's role. Attachment is also a bond that promotes exploration and gives confidence to venture forth, which is often the father's role.

Bowlby's attachment theory presents that both parents are needed as attachment figures in a child's early development. We have a long way to go before our society considers fathers to be just as important as mothers, but each step is a step closer. A successful future depends on children having secure relationships with their fathers. This means fathers being able to see their children often and being regarded as more than just financial support. Fathers are attachment figures who challenge their children and are right there with their children to explore the scary world ahead of them.

For children to grow into proficient adults, it is recommended that they first need to develop psychological security, which consists of both secure attachment and secure exploration. Researchers have defined this as confident, attentive, eager and resourceful exploration of materials or tasks, especially in the face of disappointment. Secure exploration implies a social orientation, particularly when help is needed.

Research has shown that children who grow up without consistent father involvement commit more crimes, become teenage parents more frequently and are unemployed more often than are children who grow up living with both of their biological parents full time. This is regardless of the parents' race, educational backgrounds, whether they were married at the time of their children's births or if a parent remarries. According to the research, children growing up without father involvement were also found to perform more poorly in school, use drugs more frequently and have other social problems even when controlling for generally lower income.

Mary Ainsworth and her associates experimentally defined three subgroupings of attachment associations: secure, anxious-avoidant and anxious-resistant (or ambivalent).

A secure attachment is categorized by passionate feelings of intimacy, emotional security and physical safety in the company of an attachment figure. Features that accompany a secure attachment include remarkably good communication abilities, the use of productive coping tactics and the capability to assimilate inconsistent emotions, normalize negative emotions and resolve conflicts cooperatively and constructively. Secure children show little anxiety when separated from a caregiver and develop a sense of self-worth and belongingness. Secure attachment relationships provide a safe base from which to explore the world and an affirmative model of self in relation to others.

I mean, this rings the common-sense bell more than anything else I have come across. A baby human develops in a more balanced way when both of its caregiving humans have an equal investment and bond with their offspring.

In a time where people often feel at their most comfortable within a divisive scenario where they can project their anger at the other team, it would be easy to dismiss me as being a misogynist who wants to devalue the importance and rights present to protect the wellbeing and recovery of birth mothers. A guy who is a big-head who is taking delight in mansplaining via my manosphere soapbox. A guy who is bragging to all that will listen, that speaks about himself in the third person to portray his superiority from being truly woke. Truth be told, I am just a bloke standing in front of a community, asking them to give me a fair crack at being the best partner, best parent and best dad I can possibly be.

My dad always had a snippet of wisdom to guide me through my life challenges. He is no longer with us, but his wisdom lives on. One such snippet is, 'to be old and wise, you first must be young and foolish.' I was a free-loving rascal for the majority of my youth and conformed to gender norms. I played rugby, I drank beer and I would see the icing on the cake of a night out as 'pulling' a member of the opposite sex.

The moment I saw our daughter, quite literally splash down into the world, in a bungee jumping effort from her mum's under carriage and into the birth pool I realised that I will never have a more important and special job than parenting. Especially as we were going to be raising a daughter, as my years of reckless abandonment of sewing my wild oats dawned on me. They were someone's daughters I was 'pulling.' Now that is what I call 'awoke'.

A long this journey to date, the expression 'man up' is my most detested saying. I had used it as a matter of course until I watched as my wife gave birth to our daughter, without any drugs, no gas and air and in a birth pool. That is when I woke. That is when I realised what manning up actually meant. It meant nothing. It meant bullshit. It meant accepting a predisposed cultural facade that denies the right to be an equal. An equal partner in a friendship, a marriage, a parent. My greatest responsibility from that moment on was to role model assertiveness, playfulness, kindness, safety, space to fail, space to grow, clear boundaries, effective communication, that true wealth equates to physical and mental health, equality, and absolute unconditional love.

10
Hunt for support: Take 2
Time to become a 'Union Man'

'So, as fast as I could, I went after my net. And I said, 'with my net I can get them I bet. I bet, with my net, I can get those things yet!' then I let down my net.'
Dr Seuss. The Cat in the Hat.

Prior to finding ourselves in this predicament, I have had a longstanding lack of care for unions. It gripes me that if you work for an employer and you find yourself in a position where you think you have been treated unfairly, the employer cannot support you with an independent mediator as part and parcel of protecting its staff. It really grinds my gears that we have to pay for third party, fire and theft insurance from an outside agency. Particularly annoying to me as it produces an unfair playing field where money once again determines a better life.

Yet again my principles shot me in the foot. Seeing a theme yet? At this rate I won't have any toes left! When the shit hit the fan with us I became utterly vulnerable without the legal clout of a union as it turned out. Leaving me with my pants down in the Pontypridd courtroom bumbling my way through the cross examination of a barrister with over thirty years of experience and someone who was reported to be paid in the ball park of £400 per hour.

The ironic, extra sting in the tail was that I was doing this all to spend more time with my daughter and fighting for all fathers to have the right to decide if they were in a position to spend more time with their kids. Despite my efforts to be righteous and represent the voice of the council's 'Values' and 'Equality and Diversity policy' I was continuing to punish myself. It was an example of a continuation of self-harm. Already knackered both physically and emotionally from being the best possible dad and husband I could be, while supporting vulnerable families in my daily job, I was inviting stress through my front door voluntarily. Leaving me feeling like the proverbial broken chump rather than the champ I was hoping for.

I needed help. My colleagues, who were extremely supportive and to who I will forever be grateful, suggested I join a union. I was backed into a corner and had to put my adult pants on.

I went to the resident union within my building with my tail between my legs. Low and behold, there was nothing they could do. It turned out that there was a cooling off period of a month before they could get involved. Therefore I had to truck on regardless. Like the Littlest Hobo who mosies on from place to place making friends. The only difference being, nobody wanted to be my friend.

I begrudgingly joined up with the union in case something else were to rear its ugly head in the future. SPOILER ALERT. They make a cameo later on in the story.

11
Delay, Deny, Defend

"Remember the 5 D's of dodgeball: Dodge, duck, dip, dive and dodge."
   - Patches O'Houlihan

At the time of writing, I am a member of the Youth Justice Service team. (As you will come to learn, the Sword of Damocles is teetering over my noggin). The nature of our team is to help young people and their families cope with either being in trouble with the legal system for breaking the law, or they have been referred into our service on a preventative basis to encourage them to steer away from harmful or 'offending' behaviour. My role is the latter. Our team, along with Children's Services and the Youth Service are anomalies within the behemoth structure that is Powys County Council. The vast majority of departments within The Authority provide less empathetic and supportive roles.

The folks in my team are drawn to the profession to make a positive difference to young people and their families' lives. We are definitely not drawn into the profession for the money. Definitely not. At the very core of our work is the skill-set of developing trust, respect, and rapport with young people and families who need some support. The best way of establishing this is by actions. The things we say are only words unless we give them some tangible meaning. We achieve this by being a role model with a moral compass. In my opinion, it is as simple as that. Honesty, clarity, and integrity are the pillars of a successful intervention. Which is why I have found this whole process so incredibly frustrating. The absence of acknowledgement, openness, and moral accountability continues to be a cultural tattooed template for my employers. Given the short tenures and the trend of rewarding failure up in the upper echelon cloud of the council, it is no wonder there are at worst immoral practices and at best a lackadaisical appreciation of the 'Council Values.'

The best managers I have known started at the grass roots, the front door, the coal face. They have tasted the reality, they have had dirty nails from getting stuck in and as a result they retained their principles. Other managers, sooner or later, gradually slide on their leather gloves and morph into the tried and tested template of an employee with blinkered career aspirations. You know the type. The ones who have lost their once tight grip of their morals to ensure they can continue to spend to their inflated means to keep their large mortgages and top-of-the-range motors.

This is never more glaring than when senior managers lower themselves from their cushy offices and visit us minions on the ground for 'A day in the life' of a team at the coal face. Due to the facts that the majority of young people who come into our service are either ashamed, pissed off, or have taken a leap of uncomfortable faith to confide in a trusted Youth Justice Service caseworker, it has taken substantial time to build up a rapport and an element of trust in us. By sending in a suited and booted senior manager to sit in and watch our appointments like a naughty monkey in a zoo enclosure is as short-sighted as Mr McGoo being employed as a commercial pilot. The whole idea stinks of a PR spin and a tick-box exercise.

'Meow, the last few paragraphs were a bit bitchy,' I hear you say. Well, I needed to provide a relevant example of how utterly detached and ineffective the shiny cogs are when compared to us rusty ones. We have all heard the expression, 'I am just a number', with regards to being an employee at a large company. The following example shines a light on how much our Local Authority (and LAs as a whole) are in dire need of reform in order for them to be effective and in keeping with contemporary life and needs.

As the attempted ACAS mediation between us and The Authority proved. There was as much chance of an open dialogue and a narrative that was in keeping with the 'Council Values' as a successful blind date between a vegan and a cannibal. We had two options. Give up, wave goodbye to all the stress and accept that being a dad means being marginalised. Or, apply to the Employment Tribunal in the hope of addressing the disparity of parental provisions between genders and for biological dads in particular via a Judge's decision. This would be a very short story if we chose the former.

The Employment Tribunal application form was relatively straightforward, and we hoped this would bode well for the future (if our application was to be accepted) with regards to limited legal jargon and therefore being easy to understand. I naively thought that there was no need to worry about starting the ball rolling, as the social injustice was so obvious that I was nigh on guaranteed to get support from somewhere relevant along the way.

Here comes the kick in the teeth. Brace yourself. With the Employment Tribunal confirming in writing that there would be a Full Hearing for Price v Powys County Council regarding a claim of both indirect and direct sex discrimination set for January 2019.

For clarity, the following definitions are taken from ACAS's website.

Indirect Discrimination.

Can occur where a workplace rule, practice or procedure is applied to all employees, but disadvantages those of a particular sex.

An employee or job applicant claiming indirect discrimination must show how they have been personally disadvantaged, as well as how the discrimination has or would disadvantage other employees of the same sex.

Direct Discrimination.

Is when someone is treated differently and not as well as other people because of their sex. Treating someone 'less favourably' because of:

- their own sex (ordinary direct discrimination)

I evidenced the aforementioned by using the examples of the thirteen weeks' processing time of my Shared Parental Leave in comparison with Maternity Leave and Adoption Leave requests, and by comparing the more favourable provisions available to adoptive parents.

My employers played their hand and here is how it flopped down…

Remember, remember, the fifth of November. It is a date that will not be forgotten anytime soon by me. It was a deadline given to me by the Employment Tribunal to send my employers my written 'List of Documents' that I will be referring to at the Employment Tribunal Hearing in Carmarthen on July 14th, 2019. I studiously established a list of a dozen pertinent documents which outlined my grievance and sent it to the Professional Lead of Employment Services and the Professional Lead - Human Resources Management and Development, Human Resources, Development and Health and Safety Service. The subject for the email was: 'Price v Powys County Council. Case No – 1601332/2018. List of documents to be referred to at the Employment Tribunal.'

My email dated November 5th, 2018 opened with:

'Below is a list of 12 documents that I wish to refer to at the hearing on January 14th, 2019, due to their relevance in our case of discrimination (be it direct and/or indirect) and inequality due to my male gender. The list is as follows.'

Now, I was confident then and am still confident today in stating that I made my position unambiguous and categorically clear. I had a professional, succinct, and polite response from the latter mentioned Professional Lead sharing: 'Thanks for your email and the information.'

As far as I was concerned, my responsibility was met and all was above board so to speak. Or so I thought…

On the 7th of November 2018, our daughter Eliza was three months old. My wife and I were finding our feet with childcare and parental responsibilities as a whole and we were satisfied that we could temporarily park the whole grievance issue and focus on us. An email landed in my work inbox the like of which I have never experienced before, with regards to how gobsmacked it made me (something I grew to be desensitised to along this journey, I should add). At 12:53 p.m., I received an email from the Professional Lead of the Legal Department. It stated:

'They had not received any paperwork confirming that a claim has been made, and my email came as quite a shock. They added that they had not filed a response as they were not aware of the claim.

'They respectfully asked for a judge to consider a respectful request of a short extension to file their response.'

Say what! I was flummoxed, and I will tell you for why. On the 16th of October 2018 at 12:26 p.m., I sent an email to the first of the three Professional Leads (what they were leading at this point was a tad baffling) stating the following 'Subject': 'Employment Tribunal's 'Notice of a Claim' for January 14th 2019 re Discrimination experience with Shared Parental Leave.'

Within the body of the email I stated:

'I am emailing you, as was requested by the Employment Tribunal, to indicate a 'Notice of a Claim' (to be sent no later than October 22nd, 2018) in preparation for the hearing scheduled to take place on January 14th, 2019.'

As a ruddy stickler for clarity I added:

'If there is anyone else within Powys County Council who you feel should be made aware of this 'Notice of a Claim' you have my explicit consent to forward this email to those aforementioned people.'

The Professional Lead very professionally, politely, and succinctly replied with:

'Dear Barry,

'I acknowledge receipt of your email today, the content of which is noted.

'Kind regards.'

So to put this gratingly annoying part of this whole grievance campaign into a succinct and clear way as possible.

I informed them in writing, as directed to by the Employment Tribunal on the 16th of October, that there was going to be an Employment Tribunal Hearing on January the 14th 2019. Twenty one days later, I sent the aforementioned Professional Leads my documents. Two days later the Lead of Legal at the council shared this was the first they have ever heard of my claim. There was a twenty three day window between the dates of October the 16th until November the 7th from when they were informed to do absolutely nothing. To this day, we are still on the fence as to whether this was because of utter incompetence or because of a dark, evasive 'delay, deny, and defend' strategy. Either way, it was unprofessional, lacklustre, and utterly ridiculous.

We naively figured that as we had written apologies from the following, we would be the catalyst for something positive and something that would benefit parents across my employee-hood and beyond. The welcomed apologies were as follows:

Human Resources Business Partner (£40,906 per year in Wales according to www.indeed.co.uk).

'I wanted to write to you to confirm that there are points in your email, that are very much accepted and lessons will be learnt in terms of the process around Shared Parental Leave. Unfortunately, **we can't change or interpret the legislation differently** and therefore, in this case would not be able to provide you with any different estimated figures or response.

'I would like to apologies for any undue delay that may have been caused and very much hope that this has not caused you any stress, particularly around the due date of your baby.'

The gesture of this apology was duly noted. What really grinds my gears until this day is the odd perpetual narrative that: 'We can't change or interpret the legislation differently.'

The oddness stems from the succinct statement within the Shared Parental Leave policy which points out that 'some employers offer enhanced pay'. The Welsh Government and the National Health Service decided off their own backs to 'interpret the legislation differently' within Wales and offer their employees enhanced pay when they go on Shared Parental Leave. Odd. Very odd and very much in stark contrast to their Council Values and Vision 2025.

The Professional Lead Employment Services (according to their own website regarding recruiting a Professional Lead earns £58,138-£62,790 per year) shared:

'I wish to echo REDACTED apologies on behalf of Employment Services, particularly concerning the 3 month delay in obtaining the required response in respect of Statutory Shared Parental Leave eligibility and calculations. I will be addressing this with the Payroll section to ensure that such requests are dealt with promptly, to enable parents to consider their options at the earliest possible opportunity.

'To be open and honest, I believe this is the first time that an employee has opted for Shared Parental Leave and it has regrettably highlighted issues within the council approved policy. As a result, both myself and REDACTED will work in conjunction with REDACTED and their HR colleagues to ensure that the policy is more explicit around entitlement to payments, also raising the additional points that you have made.'

It was glaringly obvious how little the Shared Parental leave policy had been promoted. It came into play across the United Kingdom in 2015 and here I was in 2018 without a clue as to what the entitlements were. I had stupidly bought into the subconscious propaganda of what an amazing and progressive employer this council was to work for and assumed equality would be a prerequisite of any parental provisions.

Now here is a classy example of how to be honest, humble, supportive, and professional. Following is my line manager's response to the email apologies:

'Following this train of email, I appreciate the apology and acknowledgement that you have offered Barry and Laura.

'I do, however, want to convey my disappointment on behalf of Barry and Laura, and also as a manager of a team in trying to plan for Barry's absence. Barry is a highly regarded, professional and dependable member of the Youth Justice Service. Rather than rewarding his dedication and commitment with a similar response to his request for support, I feel that we have let him down at one of the most pivotal points of his and Laura's life. In a climate where teams are being asked for advice on addressing the challenging issue of staff retention, one of our most reliable and creative members of staff has been left in an unnecessarily stressful predicament.

'I can see that Barry and Laura are grateful for your apology and I do not wish to disturb this process beyond registering my sadness at the situation.'

In my opinion, my line manager has revealed what a class act he is here, and his response is akin with the Council Values. I felt valued as an important cog in our team's machine and if that could be the culture across the board, what a fantastically attractive and powerful place Powys County Council, and Local Authorities in general, would be to work with. Note the use of the words 'work with', and not 'work for.'

My opinion is justified by the presentation of the evidence of my experience to date, that the aforementioned incompetence of the 'Peter Principle' is well and truly embedded within the upper management structure of my employers. The irony of having the salaries of 'Professional Leads' and acting in an unprofessionally misleading way is mind-blowing. I am not trying to throw these few individuals under the proverbial bus here. I am just revealing a snapshot of how dire the Leads and Senior Managers are allowed to be. That is not to say there have never been any professional leaders in these posts. I met one once. Back in 2013. They were not in post very long. I can only imagine that they realised they were not a good fit and left the pastures of Powys County Council to work for a company more suited to their skillset.

With a specific lens over the dropped ball of the whole twenty-three-day debacle, nobody was individually held to account. If they were, I was not a party to it. Interestingly, an individual was held to account with regards to the thirteen-week delay concerning the time taken to inform us of what I was entitled to on Shared Parental Leave. Was it the Chief Executive? A Head of Service? A Senior Manager? A Professional Lead? An elected Portfolio Holder? Or, a Line Manager? No. Don't be silly. It was an office Worker Bee whose act would be labelled as a 'human error' further along in this journey. Funny how this lowly scapegoat was hung out to dry, and the shop was well and truly shut when the upper echelon were responsible for an almighty balls-up. By the absence of accountability being shared with us and the parties involved, they continue to plod along on their inflated salaries with an air of untouchability. Not in keeping with the Council Values whatsoever. This is a perfect opportunity to point out the clear social loafing of the individual 'Leads' involved. As mentioned, this is a phenomenon by which individuals exert less effort as part of a collective than they would have if they were the one solely responsible.

The thing that really hit home in terms of the power imbalance with regards to a little person trying to get justice against a corporation was the fall out of Powys County Council's Legal Lead's email to request a postponement for them to respond. Especially in the light of me handing over every single relevant document and grievance I had to the council via my grievance emails, followed by my Notice of Hearing email and finally my List of Documents. If this was a game of poker, I had metaphorically been dealt my hand, I had turned my cards over and then slid them across to them, whilst their cards were held tightly against their chest. It was utter bollocks. The result being that, through absolutely no fault of my own, the Employment Tribunal Hearing was postponed. Here is the kicker. It was not delayed for one month, or two months, or even three months. No, no. It was postponed for nigh on eight months. It was originally booked in for Carmarthen Court on January 14th 2019 and actually went ahead on September the 6th 2019 at Pontypridd Court. True story. The 'delay' strategy was established. There are dozens of other equally frustrating and similar faux-pas by them prior to the ET Hearing. They are lying in wait in a later chapter.

On the plus side, it gave me more time to explore support at the very least, or to gain legal representation at the very best. Or so you might think.

In my David versus Goliath quest, it was now becoming patently evident that I was going to need a bigger catapult.

12
Hunt for Support: Take 3
The Citizens' Advice Bureau

'Someone is sitting in the shade today because someone planted a tree a long time ago.'
   Warren Buffet.

What does a guy have to do to get a catapult around here? I had tried and failed with enlisting a union and a meaningful ACAS mediation. Where next? Well, the glaring facts were, I was a citizen and very much in need of some advice. Where better to start looking than the Citizens' Advice Bureau? Third time's a charm! It was surely going to be one giant leap for dads, and one giant leap for parent-kind! The snowball was lobbed and airborne. Our control of the controllable left my grasp the second I had let go of that snowball. The Employment Tribunal application was accepted and the ever-accelerating little snowball was rolling off-piste, down the snowy mountain side, growing in size with every rotation and careening mercilessly towards a shiny, ivory towered cabin courthouse in the valley below. We needed a break. And fast. After all, dignity always prevails...

What is this Citizens' Advice Bureau I hear you ask? It was one of those agencies I had seemed to have always been aware of, but never felt the urge to darken their door. Until now. The Citizens' Advice Bureau's website shares that it is:

'We give people the knowledge and confidence they need to find their way forward – whoever they are, and whatever their problem.'

'Our network of charities offers confidential advice online, over the phone, and in person, for free.'

With regards to its legal branch, the website shares:

'As a member of British society you have rights and responsibilities.

'Having a job is an essential part of most people's lives. When you are in work, you can be faced with many difficult issues, so it is essential to know what your rights are.'

Finally, we found the justice firepower we needed. Our dipping confidence was escalating again. My wife and I were citizens in need of some good old-fashioned pieces of advice. Like a beacon of illumination from a lighthouse off a gloomy and misty coastline with a storm forecast to hit. I called our local Brecon CAB branch to explain our situation for the umpteenth time, and a helpful woman signposted me to their anti-discrimination branch in Newport, South Wales. This was going to be it. I could feel it in my bones. Finally, we would get the expert support we so desperately needed. Surely, this time, Stella was about to get her groove back.

I was signposted to a very calm, steady, deliberately spoken man who listened to me explain our scenario (again) and he asked for all the relevant documents. To make a judgement as to whether he could help us he required the Equality and Diversity policy, Grievance policy and The Authority's Values. I sent them over as quickly as humanly possible. After all, this was not my first rodeo. It was my umpteenth plus one and my chaps were starting to chafe.

Serendipity popped up to mock us yet again on January

14th, 2019, the date on which our ET Hearing was originally due to take place. On this day the CAB's discrimination specialist emailed me with the conclusion of his investigation into our case, entitled 'Summary of Facts'. The sub section 'Our Advice' shared: 'An employer is not obliged to pay any more than these amounts to either natural or adoptive parents. An employer may provide additional payments if it chooses to.'

Examples of employers who choose to offer additional payments are the NHS, the Welsh Government, Vodafone, and Aviva.

The CAB's concluding remarks were:

'Our funding rules only allow us to take on cases where:
- There has likely been discrimination, under the Equality Act 2010
- There is a reasonable prospect of us helping resolve your complaint
- There is enough financial value to justify ongoing assistance on your file

'We regret to inform you that we will be unable to assist you further in this matter because there is not a likely prospect of success and as the law is at the moment there does not seem to be unlawful discrimination.

'We realise this will be disappointing for you but we hope you appreciate that we have a duty to advise our clients objectively and realistically based on what the law says, and not on what we would like the law to say.'

And the rollercoaster ride continued.

Despite my employers treating me like a chump and treating me less favourably because of my testicles, the CAB door had closed. The last bullet point of 'there is enough financial value to justify ongoing assistance' was an eye opener. We were coming at this emotionally with our 'greater good' hats on and apparently this is not how the justice system works.

We still had time and optimism on our hands. Albeit waning like a polar bear in a sauna. We needed support and, after all, necessity is the mother of invention.

13
Hunt for Support: Take 4 Charity Begins at Home (Insurance)

'If you can go out there and stand up for what it is you believe in no matter how many times you are knocked down, in the end the swinging of your own blows will exhaust them.'
  Erin Brockovich.

We were beginning to believe that the scales of justice were royally fu*ked and it was going to take a miracle for us to gain the luxury of a legal eagle's swagger alongside us. As most great ideas formulate in my time, it came over a cup of tea. My wife pointed out that she was sure that our home insurance covered any legal fees that came our way. Finally! A breakthrough. I know what you are thinking, 'Slow down Schumacher, we've been here before.' And low and behold you would be correct. I called the company, explained our situation for the umpteenth and first time. I sent my documents, again, and they mulled over our case. Now, their assessment, just like the CAB, is not a process of assessing justice. No, no. It assesses if the case is financially viable given the precedents that are currently set. How does justice get served by this barrier being placed in front of any new precedents being set? The company shared that given the precedents that are currently in place we did not meet their forty percent success threshold. Hopes dashed, again.

Alas, the Human Rights Act (1998) states in *'Article 6: Right to a fair trial.'* You have the right to a fair and public trial or hearing if a public authority is making a decision that has an impact upon your civil rights or obligations.

In this context, your civil rights and obligations are those recognised in areas of UK law such as family law and employment law (relevant and pertinent information taken from www.equalityhumanrights.com).

By representing myself, without any legal experience or knowledge of legal practise, at the ET Hearing against a seasoned barrister, there was no chance of a fair trial. My civil rights were breached and I could not afford to pay for legal representation. The question as to whether my employers were incompetent or implementing the 'Delay, Deny, Defend' strategy was still a riddle, wrapped in a mystery, inside an enigma, behind a veiled illusion of cohesion, within a steaming pile of bullshit. Either way, a fair trial was not in our stars. I had no other option than to have a crack at the title on my own.

14
Going for Gold

'During this fight, I've seen a lot of changing, in the way you feel about me, and in the way I feel about you. In here, there were two guys killing each other, but I guess that's better than twenty million. I guess what I'm trying to say, is that if I can change, and you can change, everybody can change!'
　　Rocky Balboa, Rocky IV.

The following is a snapshot of the eleven documents I relied upon in an attempt to prove that my protected characteristic of sex was both directly and indirectly discriminated against at an Employment Tribunal Hearing. Think of this as a guide of how not to take on Goliath, if like me you are legally unqualified and inexperienced. I see this as an example of a naive and hopeful attempt, by myself, to explain and evidence to the judge and the respondents (The Authority) as to how I was discriminated against. I want to emphasise the word 'naive' because I was completely and utterly unsupported despite my catalogued attempts of acquiring legal/professional backing. My daily job is to support young people and families by tailoring intervention plans to encourage positive choices and gaining a realisation of the consequences of their actions. A world away from pretending to be a legal eagle. To emphasise the disparity between my efforts against a barrister and the respondent's in-house Legal Department, I was Bob Ross stepping into the UFC Octagon against Iron Mike Tyson, with nothing but my easel, curls, and pastel paint set. Think of it as an old, bobbly wool sweater-vest versus a suit of armour. Or a rabbit with myxomatosis versus a peckish T-Rex. Or my swift missionary to their tantric marathon. Or – well, you get my point. I was royally f*cked!

My argument, which led to an eventual whitewash (SPOILER ALERT) defeat is summarised by the following document headings:

Price v Powys County Council for discrimination because of my gender and role as an expectant father.

1) Outline of complaint.

As a biological father I have been treated less favourably as a male than biological mothers and adoptive parents employed by Powys County Council, evidenced by the enhanced pay offered to mothers on the Maternity Leave policy and the fact that Adoption Leave policy users have the same rights as set out in the Maternity Leave provisions.

By the respondents suggesting that some employers will offer enhanced shared parental pay we were misled into thinking it was a possibility for us. The respondents have since categorically told us that there is no scope for any enhanced pay via the Shared Parental Leave policy.

I evidenced this by quoting directly from the Shared Parental Leave policy and the Supporting Working Parents Policy, the 'progressive' Council Values, which claim to champion equality for its employees and the Vision 2025.

Via two Freedom of Information requests to Powys County Council, I have evidenced that I was treated less favourably as a male via the Shared Parental Leave policy (my only option as a biological father), demonstrated by our thirteen-week wait to hear back about my request when the average time taken to process for Maternity Leave was six weeks and Adoption Leave was three weeks.

The Shared Parental Leave policy, introduced in 2015, which was proven unfit for purpose in our case. This demonstrates that there is an institutionalized culture of gender bias against the rights and expectations of the biological father. Secondarily, the catalogue of failings by the respondents to meaningfully liaise with ACAS, their missed deadlines, and their failure to meet the Employment Tribunal's requirements for the planned hearing in July 2019. Demonstrating the lack of desire by the respondents to make amends or address their cultural failings of inequality towards biological fathers.

2) Email correspondence between myself, my manager, Human Resources, Pay Roll and Employment Services regarding our grievances.

The respondents apologised for their failings and shared that major lessons were learnt with regards to similar future requests and suggested that the councils Shared Parental Leave policy is amended to be more explicit in outlining entitlements to pay. With all due respect, it is almost a year later (summer 2019), and the Shared Parental Leave policy that we were guided by is still present and no amendments have been made. Therefore, it appears that some of the apologies were hollow and tokenistic given that no literal changes have occurred within the Shared Parental Leave policy. Namely, stating that some employers can offer enhanced shared parental leave and the Supporting Working Parents policy still states how

Adoption Leave follows the same provisions as set out in the Maternity Leave policy. The Shared Parental Leave policy does not follow the same provisions set out in the Maternity Leave policy. Elected adoptive parents have not experienced the physical and psychological effects of pregnancy and child birth, therefore it is discriminative to offer adoptive parents enhanced provisions and support when myself, a biological father on shared parental leave, is not entitled to the provisions offered to biological mothers and elected adoptive parents.

We consider the response to our complaint of sexual discrimination by the Professional Lead of Human Resources and Development to be confusing, lacking clarity, and very final. There is no mention in the email of an appeal process, an option of seeking independent support from ACAS or the resident union rep in my county council building if we were unhappy with his response, and the lack of an offer of a face-to-face meeting, to ensure there was absolute clarity in order to find closure.

3) Comparing the Shared Parental Leave with the Adoption Leave/Maternity Leave policies.

A more in-depth revelation of how less favourably I, as a biological father, was treated by the respondents when compared to mothers and adoptive parents. Highlighted as follows:

'OMP/OAP Occupational Maternity Pay / Occupational Adoption Pay – the element of pay that the Council makes provision for over and above the statutory minimum; it is subject to at least 1 year's continuous service in local government at the 11th week before the EWC.'

Paragraph 5.2 states that 'The adopter who has opted to

be the child's adopter for the purpose of taking statutory adoption leave is entitled to the same provisions as laid out in the maternity provisions.'

Paragraph 4.1 states that 'The right to maternity leave has no continuous service requirements and employees are entitled to take up to 26 weeks of Ordinary Maternity Leave (OML) and up to 26 weeks of Additional Maternity Leave (AML).'

The key point here is that the EAT decision in *Mr M Ali v Capita Customer Management* does not apply in respect of an adoptive parent. This case stated that the purpose of maternity leave for a woman who has given birth is her health and well-being following pregnancy, confinement and childbirth. It is not based on the care of the child. Quite simply, this does not apply in relation to the adoption of a child. The entitlement of adoptive parents, therefore, is based on the care provisions of the child. As a result, it is appropriate for us to claim the same entitlement on the basis of the aforementioned policy with Shared Parental Leave.

4) Freedom of Information requests to Powys County Council re Maternity Leave and Adoption Leave.

Powys County Council's compliance team confirmed that the average time taken to process Adoption Leave requests is three weeks and the average time taken to process Maternity Leave requests is six weeks. Our Shared Parental Leave request took thirteen weeks. Sadly, it would have taken longer if my line manager hadn't escalated it to the upper management employees of the Human Resources, Payroll and Employment Services.

5) Challenging the Court of Appeal's recent judgement in relation to our case specifically.

In order to achieve equality for marginalised fathers who are employees at Powys County Council, there needs to be an option on par with that of mothers and adoptive parents. The Shared Parental Leave should complement and not undermine the rights of working mothers in order for equality in parental roles to be established. If the mother returns to work after two weeks of childbirth why can't the father/partner be able to claim the untaken occupational enhanced pay the mother was entitled to.

The Court of Appeal in relation to the Ali and Hextall cases did not have Adoption Leave included as a comparator and therefore the respondents cannot compare their claim to mine, as they are different.

The lack of acknowledgement that the father's bond with the new-born is equally as important as the mother's.

6) Findings of the Welsh Assembly Government's 'Work it Out: Parenting and Employment in Wales, July 2018.'

The report highlighted flexible working, childcare, and culture change is needed in Wales to achieve gender equality at work. The report states gender inequality is not a new phenomenon, and Wales needs bold action to deliver real and lasting change. The report quotes on page twenty-eight 'Fair work' should mean equal workplaces, where people have opportunities to progress in their careers while managing their caring responsibilities, without discrimination.

7) County Council's Equality and Diversity policy.

The statement that 'The Council is fully committed to complying with the Equality Act 2010' is highly ironic in my case. I have yet to experience any commitment to equality regarding my gender or role as a father in our case.

There is a systemic failure within the culture of Powys County Council in recognising its responsibility to promote the options available, and to provide equality and diversity for male employees (whose only avenues to co-parent were the less favourable options via Shared Parental Leave and Additional Paternity/Partner Leave).

Given my experiences, I would argue that the 'values' that underpin the culture of Powys County Council are not currently fit for purpose regarding the rights of the father. A 'proactive attitude' is nowhere to be seen in my case as the true underpinning values of the respondents are evidently outdated, create a gender bias, and appear to subscribe to the obsolete stereotypes of bygone generations (i.e. mothers being caregivers to the children while the father is a breadwinner).

8) Powys County Council's Values and Vision 2025.

Whatever the reasons for the obvious discrimination taking place, it cannot in good conscience be concluded that fathers have anywhere near the appropriate parity of support from the respondents when it comes to parenting.

It is clear from the aforementioned evidence in my case that neither one of the 'values' are present in our situation, evidenced by the delays from Human Resources, Employment Services, and Pay Roll regarding our Shared Parental Leave query and reinforced again, when there was a failure by Powys County Council to collaborate with ACAS in a timely manner, giving us no alternative other than to apply to the Employment Tribunal to continue our challenge.

9) The European Union's policies regarding sexual discrimination and the Human Rights, Article 8 – Right to

respect for private and family life, and Article 14 – Prohibition of discrimination.

As pointed out in the 'EU DIRECTIVE OF THE EUROPEAN PARLIAMENT AND OF THE COUNCIL on work-life balance for parents and carers and repealing Council Directive 2010/18/EU'. This provision 'should' encourage fathers to take advantage of the parental leave system and thus lead to mothers not staying away from the labour market for too long. Currently, biological fathers such as myself are hamstrung from choosing to take the Shared Parental Leave or Additional Paternity/Partner Leave options because they are financially unviable. As they are the only avenues for myself to access parental leave support from my employer, there is no other alternative. Therefore, I am completely let down by a system that is clearly not fit for purpose and marginalises biological fathers as a result.

As for the breaches of my Human Rights. Article 8 'The right to respect for family life' is pertinent in our case in relation to the protection of my family's health and how we wanted to parent. (Mental health in particular as a result of the additional stress caused by both the failings of the respondent's policies and due to the thirteen week delay we had to wait which was considerably longer than both Maternity Leave and Adoption Leave averages added together.) My morals and the protection of my rights and freedoms were also breached as a result.

Article 14 'Prohibition of Discrimination' is applicable to our challenge, as I have been treated less favourably because of my gender, concerning the Shared Parental Leave entitlement of Statutory Pay, in comparison to Maternity Leave's Enhanced Pay and the more favourable provisions offered to Adoption Leave (Adoption/Maternity Pay) on par with Maternity Leave.

10) Recent studies re post-natal pressure on fathers.

This section is relevant to my claim as it highlights a modern, up to date, and relevant take on the psychological pressures new fathers experience. Given the recent Court of Appeal's summation that the mother's bond with her baby is prioritised over that of the father, this section is especially relevant regarding the hurt feelings I have experienced in addition to the psychological and physical strain of co-parenting our first baby. The respondents have exacerbated the pressure upon me with their lack of willingness to liaise with ACAS, forgetting to share that they had a Notice of a Hearing in writing from me, which they failed to share with their own legal team. This, as mentioned previously, derailed the whole proceedings and dragging this whole ordeal on for several months, at a time when I was already experiencing an unprecedentedly high level of stress in my daily life.

In addition, the respondent's lack of willingness to achieve meaningful discussions with the appointed ACAS conciliator was disrespectful, unprofessional, ignorant to the cause of marginalised biological fathers, and was unacceptable.

11) Claimant Witness Statement.

Without forcing the point, the several missed deadlines and lack of care and willingness to acknowledge my claim shown in general by the respondents from day one has been a complete fiasco of inefficiency. Unfortunately, the additional stress has soiled the experience of the whole first year of parenting for my wife and myself.

Case closed!

So there we have it. My list of documents that I relied upon at the eventual ET Hearing. The list which I shared with the respondents on November the 5th, 2018. Ten months before the eventual ET Hearing. What an un-fricking believable shower of caci-poo-poo.

The question remains whether the respondent's actions were a genuine shambles beyond belief, or was this their attempt at a 'Delay, Deny, Defend' power move in an effort to crush my spirits and therefore my case? The truth is out there.

15.
The Great 'Bundle' Bungle

"There's an old saying in Tennessee — I know it's in Texas, probably in Tennessee — that says, fool me once, shame on — shame on you. Fool me — you can't get fooled again."
    George W. Bush

Representing myself in a discipline which is completely alien is hard enough. Throw in the failure to encourage and entice outside agencies, such as the CAB and a Union, to support me along the way made for an even tougher escapade. I would best describe the following two chapters as a 'How NOT to guide' in taking on The Man. Latter chapters are more of a 'How to guide.' The phoenix needed to feel the heat before it could be reborn! The following quote by Denis Waitley epitomises our social justice expedition: 'Failure should be our teacher, not our undertaker. Failure is delay, not defeat. It is a temporary detour, not a dead end. Failure is something we can avoid only by saying nothing, doing nothing and being nothing.'

Moreover, the Employment Tribunal itself is flawed when it comes to accommodating laypeople who are representing themselves. At the very least there should be a handy checklist (in layperson's language) to guide us through the dense forest of bracken and deadwood, which is the practice of law. One of only two luddite practices (the other being estate agencies) who have rigidly remained in the dark ages by digging their heels in reluctantly to refuse any sort of modernisation akin with contemporary life. More delays, more drudgery, more confusion only drags out proceedings, which ensures that they continue to be the experts, and ensures that the maximum amount of juice can be squeezed out of every lemon that steps across the deadwood threshold and ventures blindly into the bracken and blackthorns.

I am one of those lemons. At the outset, I was a ripe and zesty lemon. Ripe and ready for anything. After almost two years of being squeezed, I am a husk of dry pith, strewn across the ground of an abandoned lemon tree orchard, decomposing with the rest of my once zesty lemon brothers and sisters. And all because I am a nice bloke, standing up for the rights of all parents within our shires. An admirable conquest, which shines a light on how extremely deep-seated gender bias is within the UK when it comes to the lack of equality present within parental rights.

The best metaphor I can muster for representing myself within the employment tribunal process is volunteering to walk solo across a barren desert with only one bottle of water and a calendar as company. Oh, and the bottle of water has a hole in it. Along the arid ramble, I headed out in a direction I hoped would be correct. All the while water dripped slowly and consistently from my bottle onto the sands below. Certain deadline dates were circled on my calendar, and I knew I had to have met certain requirements by said dates, which I made sure I did. On said dates I would look up at the sky to see if there was any sign of the vulture (team of vultures and a barrister vulture in my case). Unfortunately, the only consistencies I experienced on my desert expedition were that:

a) my water was running out, b) I met my deadlines on the circled dates on the calendar, c) I was all alone, every single uncertain step of the way, and d) the vultures were always late.

To this day, I am in a quandary as to whether the vultures were that disorganised and inefficient which resulted in them being consistently late. Or was it their sly ploy to grind me down to a sorry standstill in the hope that I would make a U-turn and retreat back to the safety of anonymity and abandon my legal challenge. Either way, the Employment Tribunal would benefit from adopting a supportive role for claimants who are representing themselves. After all, it is in their best interests to streamline the process in order to achieve clarity and efficiency, which makes their life easier too.

And that brings us nicely to the great 'Bundle Bungle.' For those of you who do not know, a 'Bundle' in relation to an Employment Tribunal Hearing is a collection of documents, which the claimant (me) and the respondents (vultures) refer to as evidence for and against the dispute. In our case, sexual discrimination. Not to be confused with the claimant's 'Submission Documents.'

A fun thing to share with you. At the hearing the judge asked me whether a certain document was for my evidence or my submission. I confidently answered 'Evidence, your honour,' and the respondent's barrister actually laughed at me. To be accurate it was more of a snigger. Still, very unwelcome, unhelpful, and very disrespectful to a bloke who was clearly paddling upstream in a wardrobe, with sausages for paddles, through choppy treacle.

The theoretical beauty of the Employment Tribunal preparation process is that both the claimant and the respondent mutually agree upon a 'Joint Bundle'. That way there is a balanced perspective where all relevant documents are present at the Employment Tribunal Hearing. Both sides of the story are wrapped up neatly in a nice little bow. Thus, making the judge's job clearer and more manageable.

A 'Bungle' is defined by the Merriam Webster dictionary as 'to act or work clumsily and awkwardly.' Or to 'Mishandle or to botch'. In my 37 years, the biggest bungle I have ever encountered began on the 22nd of August 2019, 14 days prior to the arranged Employment Tribunal Hearing. The head of the respondent's legal team responded to my email requesting some clarity on what documents should be in the joint bundle and what should be included in my submission documents. It was the first time we had liaised in the lead up as the solicitor I usually worked with was on holiday. The head's response was seemingly a breath of fresh air on a Mumbai city centre roundabout for an asthmatic jogger. He replied concisely, he used yellow highlights, and he even used red writing to confirm what will be in the Joint Bundle. Here is a little nod to the absurdity of proceedings. The respondent managed the Joint Bundle and I was left to trust their professionalism and efficiency, two key areas that had been lacking for everyone who had represented the respondents over the previous fourteen months. Nonetheless, there appeared to be a new Sheriff in town who filled me with confidence. The head of the legal team. How could this possibly go wrong? He literally used colourful words and he highlighted in yellow. And finally, I could relax. Or, wait for it.

Friday August the 30th 2019 came around. T-minus six days until the Employment Tribunal Hearing. Three working days before the hearing. The hefty Joint Bundle arrived in the post in the afternoon. Lovely stuff. Now, before I go on, bear in mind that my case is regarding sex discrimination and inequality. I opened the giant Joint Bundle lever arch file, which contained more pages than a braille bible. I perched myself at the kitchen table with a large mug of tea, pen and pad to hand, and inspected the bugger. To this day, I have no idea why I allowed my naivety to rear its affable head again, but it rocked up nonetheless. Despite the head confirming via email in pretty colours, the Joint Bundle was missing the Freedom of Information Requests which identified that Maternity Leave requests took six weeks on average to process, and the Adoption Leave process took three weeks on average. This was very frustrating, not only as the head confirmed it would be present in the Joint Bundle, but it also was imperative in evidencing how monumentally different my thirteen-week wait was compared with other parents.

You guessed it. There was more apparent skulduggery. In the formulation of the Joint Bundle file, the respondents did not include the 'Equality and Diversity policy' and the 'Grievance policy.' Both policies were missing. I genuinely coughed on my tea at this point. Of all the documents to omit in a sex discrimination case where a dad had a grievance which pointed out (and quoted regularly up until this date) the failings with the respondent's Equality and Diversity policy and the Grievance policy. Now, as I sat at my kitchen table, mouth hung open in disbelief, with sweet, milky tea dripping down my bearded chin, I hit my lowest ebb of faith in the respondents' ability to complete basic tasks. I never experienced such utter disbelief in all of my life. My confidence in the head finally pulling all of his side's tomfoolery together in a neat, concise, and succinct package had imploded in new lows of shoddiness. But wait, alas there is more.

At this point, my wife entered to see what my gasps were about. All I could muster was a maniacal giggle. I could not put into words how this was another balls-up in a long list of balls-ups! Just for good measure the respondents omitted their 'Values and Vision 2025', which pointed out:

'We are determined to create public services of the future that are driven by the right culture and behaviours. We will make sure our values are integral to the way we manage and recruit our staff, as our values and behaviours will guide all aspects of the way we work.

'These are:
- Progressive
- Positive
- Professional
- Open
- Collaborative.'

According to the Collins Dictionary, the word 'Progressive' is 'Someone who is progressive or has progressive ideas has modern ideas about how things should be done, rather than traditional ones.'

An argument which was absent from our mutually agreed Joint Bundle. What to do next? There was nothing I could do for two more days. It was the weekend and no one was available until Monday morning. Deceitfulness? Carelessness? Or ineptitude? I will never know. Without an answer to this, I could not fairly project my frustration on The Head or The Authority. After all, you cannot blame Mr McGoo for scraping someone's car door in a supermarket carpark. Shoddy is what shoddy does.

T-minus four days.

The weekend had passed. My gobsmacked frustration and

disbelief had subsided and returned to a more helpful air of positivity and hope. Despite the debacle of calamity to date, at the very core of my grievance was a righteous and obvious example of sex discrimination. A win at the Employment Tribunal Hearing would set the wheels of social justice in motion to give families a gender-neutral right to share their parental leave on a level playing field and in a manner which suits their unique family dynamic. I was firing up a flare from a disaster zone to highlight to the cavalry that we need you. Progressive change was afoot. Surely. After all, ever since this whole palaver began, I have religiously adhered to the rule of the 'seven Ps'. Prior Planning and Preparation Prevents P*ss Poor Performance. I have met every deadline. I have provided everything that was asked of me without any help (despite my regular May Day calls to various 'supportive' agencies), and we championed openness and clarity from day one.

Monday morning rolled around and I was as keen as a malnourished crow hovering over a worm's hole. Then bang, I made my pre-planned assertive and clear phone call to the Employment Tribunal. I asked whether the documents included in Joint Bundles were always decided upon by the respondents? Adding that four of the essential documents I requested, documents that were agreed upon in writing by the head, were not included in the actual Joint Bundle delivered to me in the post. The very helpful Employment Tribunal office representative shared that she would discuss with the judge and get back to me. Soon after, I received a phone call from the helpful person who shared there will be an 'urgent' Preliminary Telephone Hearing with the judge on Wednesday morning for the respondents and myself. A day before the Employment Tribunal Hearing at Pontypridd Court. Cutting things awfully fine by anyone's standard.

To paint a human picture for you here. My annual leave had never, ever been so valuable. With regards to childcare, my wife and I were getting so good at juggling that we could have graduated from clown school. We needed to scrutinize every minute of my annual leave in order to ensure we could provide childcare for our daughter. My wife was self-employed so she did not have any leave to speak of. No work, no pay. Because of the Bundle Bungle, I needed to take the Wednesday morning off because of the actions of others. The cascade of perpetual disappointment in my employers continued. I had already booked the Thursday and Friday off for the two-day Employment Tribunal Hearing. Three days of leave that are of zero help for looking after and spending quality time with my baby daughter and wife.

    Wednesday came around and I was eager to hear what the judge was going to make of the respondent's continued culture of nonsensical disregard for the Employment Tribunal process. I adopted my usual pensive pose at the kitchen table. Laptop open and several documents laid out in a semi-circle, like petals around the laptop flower. I called in at 9:50 a.m., ready for the ten a.m. start as requested in writing. 9:58 a.m. came and the judge's voice landed. Polite, respectful and with an air of professional grace. In all honesty, I was hoping that her demeanour would make a Stig-like wheel spinning U-turn if and when the respondent's barrister was going to enter the conversation, and unleash holy hell upon him. Ten a.m. came and went. The judge asked her office to chase up the respondents, to no avail. Now, it is important to add here that there had been two previous Preliminary Telephone Hearings to date, both of which left me sitting in an awkward silence and chats about the weather with both the current judge and a previous judge. Both of the previous Preliminary Telephone Hearings were postponed until later in their respective days. Lo and behold, you guessed it, on the eve of the Employment Tribunal Hearing at Pontypridd Court, the barrister was not only late, he did not call in. I was asked to call back in an hour. The clusterf*ckery continued.

I called back in an hour and the legal eagle had landed. Before the 'Bundle Bungle' could be slapped about the barrister's chops by the judge. Out of left field she surprised me with an odd, curveball of a question. Bearing in mind, I could almost touch the end tip of my tether after almost fifteen months of grievance rising and wanted nothing more than to get this show on the road as soon as possible.

On average, I had spent at least two hours a day on this case over those fifteen months. Approximately nine hundred hours of my life. Nine hundred hours of an evening, in the wee hours of the night, during my baby daughter's naptimes and at my work desk during my lunch breaks. For the love of all things good and pure, surely I had sacrificed all of this time for an incredibly worthwhile reason.

The judge shared that she had in fact been a consultant for my employers in a legal capacity a few years ago. She wanted to know if I found this to be a conflict of interest and went onto share that if I did, I could request another judge to replace her, which would involve a postponement of proceedings. Twenty-two hours before we were due to sit opposite one another in a courtroom. She asks me this now. The pressure and stress had far exceeded anything I had experienced in my life to date. In hindsight, perhaps I should have played the cautious card and requested another judge. I just wanted it done. I wanted my chance to put things right. I confirmed that I did not want a delay and shared that I did not think there was a conflict of interest. The judge took note and concluded the meeting by telling the barrister that the confirmed documents must be included in the final, final Joint Bundle and handed to me tomorrow morning at the Pontypridd courthouse. That was it? Surely not? Unfortunately so. The question of 'What would the judge or respondents have done if I had acted in such a lacklustre way throughout this process?' yo-yoed back into my conscious. Had I done that, I am confident that my lack of respect for the process would have been taken note of more than that of The Authority. For some reason, The Authority appeared to be getting away with it. There was an acceptance of their ineptitude. A seemingly unconscious bias had reared its fugly head, again.

16
My day in court!
(Rabbit in the proverbial headlights)

"YOU CAN'T HANDLE THE TRUTH!"
Jack Nicholson - A Few Good Men.

Wednesday, September the 4th 2019. Court day eve.

    My daughter, wife and I went out for a relaxing pub lunch before I set off to Pontypridd in mid-afternoon. Pontypridd is only roughly one hour and twenty minutes from our house but I was not willing to make it all this way to this point and fall at the last hurdle, and a traffic delay cause me to be late for the Hearing (see the '7 Ps' from earlier). Words to live by people. With the car loaded up with my suit and overnight bag I was waved off like a gallant knight on a sacred quest for justice for the downtrodden by the two beautiful ladies in my life. I slid the automatic into 'D' and watched my girls get smaller and smaller in the rear-view mirror and I was off. Ponty here I come!

    For those of you who have been to Pontypridd, the roundabout on the edge of the town is as confusing as a smartphone to a giraffe. Nonetheless, the town was lovely and I was keen to get settled into my hotel room, get some chow and have a walk through my documents before a well-deserved early night. Nothing could dampen my evening's positive mind set. I was the master of how the rest of Wednesday was going to pan out. That was what the four thirty p.m. version of me thought. I settled in, had some grub, laid out my laptop flower and document petals on my king-sized bed, cup of tea (in a classic toddler-sized hotel cup) in hand.

I turned on my laptop and saw I had an email from the respondent's solicitor. I opened it and that was when the metaphorical torque became too much for my rails, and the mastering of the rest of my day was derailed. At 5:17 p.m., the solicitor sent the final digital version of the final, final Joint Bundle, which felt like a minor victory for Team Price. In addition, there was confirmation that they have added an additional witness for tomorrow's hearing. Up until then, there had only been one witness. Now there were two. We were requested to share our respective Witness Statements a month ago. I had done so by the requested deadline and they managed it about two weeks ago. So, here we were, fifteen hours and forty-three minutes before the hearing's kick-off and they had just informed me that they are adding a second witness and had attached the additional Witness Statement to this email. Utter clusterf*ckery incarnate. The narrative of both Witness Statements was clear. An individual employee was being thrown under the proverbial bus as the broken 'human error' link in the corporate chain.

Go Time.

Seven a.m. Thursday, September the 5th, 2019.
The first of my three phone alarms rang out as I lay,

already wide-eyed awake, in my big ole lonely hotel bed in Pontypridd. Finally, it was go time. My biggest 'adulting' challenge to date. I toyed with my fried breakfast like a toddler at a shoelace. Then I suited up, had a pep-talk with my wife over the phone and heard some supportive and inspirational babbles of advice from my daughter and left for Pontypridd court.

I will be honest, I was hopeful of carrying myself with my head held high and advertising myself as a guy who had his sh*t together and meant business. Unfortunately, on my arrival at the court I could not find any parking spaces anywhere near the court building. There was a parking barrier adjacent to the court building, which rose as a very expensive and shiny sports car neared. It drove in and disappeared around the back of the building. Time to park up and get this circus on the road I thought. The barrier was still raised so I moseyed on in and parked my little chilli red Toyota Yaris in between the shiny sports car (its alloys probably worth more than my car) and a top of the range shiny Range Rover. I had arrived at the inner sanctum and was as ready as I could possibly be. Simultaneously when I turned off my engine, a lady appeared from the building and made a beeline over to my driver's side. 'Quite the welcome,' I thought. She politely and firmly pointed out that I had parked in the judge's private car park. I made my bashful excuses and tootled back out under the barrier. I would like to say that this balls-up went against the grain of an otherwise very, very successful few days. I wish I could have said that.

Take two. I drove in a three mile loop from the courthouse to park in Sardis Road which is a stone's throw away from the back of the court. I climbed the dozens and dozens of steep steps up to the courthouse with my backpack full of documents. All the while feeling like a smaller, whiter, bearded version of John Coffey. Walking the Green Mile! After an airport style metal detector welcome, I was directed to a holding room, a pen, alongside several emotionally frazzled humans. All of whom were clearly very, very invested in their own private wars against someone or something. A mish-mash of a few eager reporters dotting amongst us war mongers. Some of us had bought into the bullsh*t expectations of donning our best suit and ties. Others were throwing up a metaphorical 'f*ck you' to the system by wearing tracksuits and trainers. Sadly, having experienced in my line of work that young offenders who go to court showing willing by dressing in a suit have a far better chance of leniency from their judge. I was a bigger version of that sheep mentality. A desperate soul, doing whatever I could to give an impression of a winner. A horse that should be backed, rather than a horse getting led into the back entrance of a glue factory.

One of many sad things I experienced in the holding pen was the clear divide. Running parallel to the pen was a series of private rooms. Each door had a narrow window where we could see the relaxed, smiling faces of the barristers and solicitors supping on their coffees without a care in the world. In fairness, if I was on around £400 per hour a bazooka could not take that smile off my face. It held up a mirror to what is wrong with society. The richer you are the better chance of justice you can afford. Smugness incarnate and personified. My employers had a legal team consisting of a Legal Lead who was a solicitor, the head of the department, and a barrister, versus me. An unqualified youth justice worker with principles. I was literally taking two days off from my day job to take on these folks and The Authority. Priceless annual leave given my family commitment I should add. A lovely clerk introduced herself to me and a suited old gent walked over and handed me the final, final, final Joint Bundle in a large yellow lever arch file. He did not introduce himself so I assumed he was an employee of the courthouse too. I thanked him and with ten minutes or so before I was called down to the courtroom I skimmed through the beast of a file and lo and behold, I had yet again been bent over and shown who was boss! Even after yesterday's telephone discussion and stern words from the judge, the promises that were made, the respondent's reputation and principles, the Joint Bundle still failed to include one of the Freedom of Information Requests specifically regarding Adoption Leave. My main comparator being Adoption Leave. Moreover, my documents literally quote the 'Council Values' from the Grievance policy from 2018. Very unhelpfully for my challenge, the respondents included the 2019 updated version of the values. All of a sudden, I felt like I had just discovered more holes in my little boat and I was about to voluntarily cross shark infested and choppy waters. I was chum. Here I was, wholeheartedly believing that I stood gallantly on the precipice of a new dawn in parental equality and my hull had been torpedoed. Again!

As I sat in the pen, pondering how best to bail the ankle-high water from my boat, a lady sitting nearby asked me if I was Barry. I thought, 'What are the chances of coming all this way and bumping into someone who knows me?' It turned out she was a journalist from my local newspaper. 'Fandabbydosey,' I thought. At least I am not on my own. We chatted briefly until the friendly court clerk from earlier announced, 'Price versus Powys County Council. We are ready for you. Follow me please.' Like an overgrown, grey haired and bearded high school pupil, I put my rucksack on, carried my giant yellow bundle of joy with two hands and walked the mile with the clerk leading the conga line, myself in the middle, and the journalist at the tail end. I saw the Joint Bundle Folder Gift Man appear from his private, comfy room adjacent to the pen exit too. Two men appeared with him who resembled a short Stan Laurel and a clean-shaven Oliver Hardy (minus the hat and 'tache). Then there were six. We were led to a closed courtroom entrance and offered a seat by the court clerk. Bar the standard 'Good mornings' we sat in silence for several minutes. I returned my wired attention to the giant file, which was perched on my lap like an anchor.

The court clerk concluded the awkward holding room silence by opening the door to the courtroom and invited us all in. The six of us entered the courtroom. No sign of any judge just yet. More suspense. Dun-dun-dun. In an act of attaining some level of warmth and respect, I poured myself a glass of water and offered the others a drink. Stan and little Laurel accepted. They were sat behind me in the middle row and my new journalist friend was sat in the back row like a naughty pupil at the back of the school bus. She was armed with a pen, pad, and looked eager to kick off. My neighbour in the front row, (who was the giver of the Joint Bundle back up in the pen) who I now deduced was the barrister, politely declined a tipple. The temporary calmness was derailed when the court clerk said 'Please stand for the judge.' It was on. Finally.

The judge, who I had spoken to during the emergency preliminary telephone hearing the previous day, was younger than I predicted and presented with an air of authority and warmth. She was flanked by two panel members. Both ladies, who apart from a hello, were mute throughout the two days. It was a little uncomfortable as they behaved as if they were on a sponsored silence and I half felt guilty for not sponsoring them. I was literally just a guy, standing in front of a girl (and her two friends), asking her to let me go halves on my baby nurturing responsibilities.

I was never told what the specific roles of the judge's two silent assistants sat on either side of her. They were the wings to her cockpit, or the testicles to her shaft. Either way, they were quieter than church mice. I will be eternally grateful to the judge for how patient she was with my cluelessness, and she remained completely respectful towards me over the two days.

Court Highlights, Day One.

Having only had hearsay experience of barristers, so no actual experience, I was prejudiced towards the beasts known as barristers. I had a prejudiced impression that they were sly, they would trip you up, they would rely on jargonized and bamboozling litigation language, would toy with you, would touch a nerve to rattle you and would have the cold emotional detachment of a sociopath. I am no longer prejudiced. If I based my opinion of all the worlds' barristers on this one experience, I would conclude that all the hearsay was accurate. Imagine an eel, a fox, a magpie, a weasel, a snake and a shark all rolled into one and dressed in a tailored suit, and that would be about it. Of course, I am being harsh here and I base this on the ridiculous notion of a system which allows such an imbalance to take place. What was all that talk about the 'right to a fair trial?' In absolute honesty, the barrister was brilliant. He did his job effectively.

Early on in the day the judge shared that she was not completely clear on my comparators in my case. I shared that I had extra copies off my documents which explained in more detail regarding the Maternity Leave and Adoption Leave policies respectively. The judge asked me if this was for 'evidence' or 'documents' and being sodden behind my ears I assumed it was evidence and I indicated so. As mentioned earlier, the barrister sniggered at my naive cluelessness. I kept cool but my hackles were raised a tad. As the barrister and the judge hashed out what comparator to agree upon, with the odd confused input from myself, the barrister took the stance of referring to me as 'him' repeatedly. The Judge referred to me as Mr Price throughout, which was nice. She gave me the illusion of playing a role in this discussion. 'Him', not so much. The hackles were a little more protrusive. The judge acknowledged that the last-minute para-trooping witness was unusual, and she asked if I was willing to allow it. Like an absolute numpty (hindsight) I agreed. 'Yeah, come on in, the more the merrier.'

Then came an experience of feeling utterly vulnerable. To give you some comparisons, I have been a master of ceremony at a friend's wedding, a best man a few times and even wrote and read my father's eulogy in front of a thousand mourners. Despite the resilience of said experiences the cross-examination was on another level of vulnerability. My ego, my passion of the past year, my love for my family and the expectations of friends, family and colleagues, were all toyed with and trodden on. Basically, I was shat on from a great height. And it felt as though it went on and on and on until I was suffocating in corporate and legal bullshit. I was the first up to the hot seat. I was trying my best to embrace my inner zen. I was consciously counting my breathing whilst focusing on the feeling in my feet of being grounded. The very first thing the barrister did, whilst continuing to refer to me as him, was to ask me to turn to a particular page in the Bundle. The file was such a beast that it took me what felt like an age to find the page, which displayed a particular email from my wife on our behalf to the respondents. This was the wily old fox's first warning shot across my bow. The email was sent post blanket apologies from the departments involved for taking thirteen weeks to process our Shared Parental Leave request, which left us in the lurch three weeks prior to the birth of our first child. In the email, my wife thanked them for their apologies. I had also made the same polite gesture in another email. The barrister hammed up his reaction as he stated confusion as to why we are even here given the resolution having already occurred. The respondents apologised and my wife had accepted it. End of in his opinion. At this point, to paint an accurate picture it is worth mentioning that the judge had her head down for the vast majority of my cross-examination, making notes. She respectfully informed me of this prior to the onslaught so that was absolutely fine. Like I had a choice. During my cross examination the barrister raised his eyebrows at occasions where I appeared to be at my most stupid and continued to refer to me as him. At one point he yawned and at another he leant back in his seat and checked the time on his shiny watch. It was at this point where my hackles burst through the back of my suit like the purple prickles on the Gruffalo's back. I asked him if I was boring him. A hammed up am-dram reaction followed from the hurt barrister, and this was acknowledged by the judge as she turned her attention from squirreling her notes to look at the poor barrister. It was at this point when I knew that if I ever had a hint of an upper hand, said appendage had been chopped off at this moment. I had lost my calmness, which was the only thing I thought would anchor me. I hoped that my attempt at zen would mean I could be as coherent and clear as possible.

The comment that will be forever etched in my memory in the whole bamboozling experience, is one which I have alluded to many chapters ago. When I caught a break and momentarily found myself in the serene eye of the storm. There was a fleetingly brief window of opportunity where I found the right words in the right order and expressed them clearly. I shared something along the lines of, 'I hope that in ten years from now there will be no need for comparator pools such as biological dads versus birth mums or biological dads versus adoptive parents. I hope that there will only be one pool. A primary carer pool known as "parent". A pool where gender is irrelevant and there will be equality in provisions for a baby's primary caregiver.'

Riding the one and only little high of the whole experience, the barrister shot me down in flames by saying 'We don't live in a perfect world, Mr Price.' Cold, succinct, decisive, and brilliant. At least he referred to me as Mr Price this time, every cloud and all that!

The one sided 'Mano-a-Mano' cross-examination ding-dong came to an end and left me in what I can only describe as a metaphorical post feverish love-making effort with excessive gusto. I was absolutely spent and as I returned to my seat I metaphorically sparked up a cigarette and felt in desperate need of a cleansing shower, as the barrister nonchalantly got dressed and made his way to the bedroom door without as much as a goodbye, or 'I'll call you.' He had ruined me.

It is safe to say that what confidence I did have was now

strewn across the courtroom floor like ashes from an urn emptied at a draughty cliff edge. Next was my time to cross-examine not one, but two of the council's witnesses. It did not go well at all, in any way, shape, or form. Their party line, despite the apologies of the leaders perched well above them in the corporate food chain hinting at them taking some responsibility, was to blame one administrative employee in one of the departments for their 'human error.' Or, as you and I would refer to them as, the scapegoat. Managerial arse covering 101 was in motion. I was asked to flick through my wedge of a file again to the email thread section where the scapegoat had shared an email with me. In this email they alluded to this being the first time a dad has requested this, and they added a 'Ha-ha' to boot which the barrister highlighted, which seemed unnecessary, unless it was for the reason of discrediting them, thus adding weight to the possible 'human error' theory. I had no issue with the 'Ha-ha' as they were just being human and it was so early on in the process that I was aware that they, like myself, were a mere rusty cog in the council machine.

When I challenged the witness by asking whether there was a lack of guidance and supervision by him, Laurel was not a happy chappy. He shared something along the lines of 'How dare you?' So that went well.

Next up was Hardy. In the history of epic, badass, table flipping 'YOU CAN'T HANDLE THE TRUTH!' courtroom battles, this cross-examination was not one of them. I actually opened with an apology as I found out that he had driven down from the very north of Powys this morning. From his body language and how he handled himself he appeared to be a genuinely nice bloke and like me, he was uncomfortable in this environment and would rather be anywhere else but here.

So all in all, a rather shitty day for Team Price. Time to go back to the hotel to have a feed and a cry.

Court Highlights, Day Two. Remedy Day.

Once again, I took my spot in the pen and waited for a number of hours before being led into the courtroom. Just like I needed some extra drama and tension. My sphincter was tauter than an industrial vice and my testes retreated to their prepubescent cul-de-sacs.

By now I was on 'cheers mate' terms with the security guards parked at the court's entrance. They took an interest in my case and as with everyone else I had spoken to, prior to yesterday's spoilsports, they shared that there is a clear inequality in parenting and they wished me well. It was a good omen, I told myself.

The clerk gave the call out and our reduced conga line consisting of her, the barrister, myself, and the stoic local reporter. When in the courtroom, awaiting the judge, the barrister looked miffed. I shook hands with him and asked if he was okay. He shared that due to the delay of our remedy hearing today, he was likely to be late for his dinner plans that night. And there lay how polar opposite our emotional attachment to the pending outcome would be.

My naivety landed when the judge and her wings of justice entered looking 'out-out ready' in their finery and make up. I honestly pondered whether this was down to a landmark precedent being set today and they were photo-ready for the awaiting press. My ponderings were utterly unfounded as the judge dropped the bomb that she and her flankers had unanimously decided that my employers had not discriminated against me directly or indirectly as a result of my gender. The

Ali case (which did not involve adoption leave provisions) was at the core of the judge's decision. As the judge broke the news, she went through legal gobbledy-goop to justify how she came to this decision. I tried to hold it together, but my bottom lip was quivering like a blue tit in a birdbath.

This whole experience had been completely alien to me. I had never been to court before and despite my firm belief that I was doing the right thing by hovering my head above the parapet, I could not help but feel I was in trouble. I have rarely been in trouble in my life. I accidentally broke a window in the high school changing room in Year Eight when I threw a rugby ball to my mate Chris who failed to catch it. That is about it. The viscosity of said atmosphere became increasingly greasy with the slickness of the barrister's seasoned patter. The oiliness of his lingo clogged up any potential social justice progress gaining any traction towards reforming the un-contemporary and stereotypical Shared Parental Leave policy and the unconscious bias against marginalised fathers. A bias which should have been relegated to Room 101 decades ago. I felt like the hapless seagull, covered beak to webbed toes in thick black, oozy oil after a spill.

Remedy aftermath.

As brushed upon earlier, the patter of the legal tongue was harder to follow than Jason Bourne at Heathrow's departure lounge. The following gives some perspective as to my point:

'Section 13 Equality Act 2010 defines direct discrimination as:

'"A person (A) less favourably than another (B) if, because of any protected characteristic, A treats B less favourably than A treats or would treat others"

'By virtue of section 13(6)(b) EqA 2010, if the protected characteristic is sex, in a case where B is a man, no account is to be taken of special treatment afforded to a woman B in connection with pregnancy or childbirth.'

'Section 19 Equality Act 2010 defines indirect discrimination in the following terms:

'"A person (A) discriminates against another (B) if A applies to B a provision, criterion or practice (PCP) which is discriminatory in relation to a relevant protected characteristic of B's.'

My mind returned to 1995, when I uttered the words 'Algebra. Pfft. I mean, honestly, when am I ever going to use that?' In September 2018. That was when.

I cannot emphasise the imbalance of power and capability between myself and the barrister. I wish I could say that I had a specific set of skills that would help me find the failings that led to social justice being taken by the shoddy Shared Parental Leave policy and unconscious gender bias. But... my specific set of skills are listening, cuddling, and drinking tea. In no way were these skills in anyway helpful today. If anything, they were a hindrance. Firstly, my listening skills were flawed as I was not fully aware what the hell was being spoken about. Secondly, nobody looked like they would welcome a cuddle from me, and thirdly, there was no tea. I was the wonky shopping trolley to the barrister's Formula One McLaren. The chipolata to the rib-eye steak. Despite this, in my heart of hearts I was convinced that my grievance would have been righteous and morally founded enough to turn a few heads. Surely, I could not lose because of my lack of adversarial skills. Surely, my grievance alone was enough to highlight how marginalised biological dads' rights are? Forget the Walking Dead. I was the Walking Dead Dad! Just a zombie wading through an oil spill, drinking tea, listening to people, and offering out free hugs.

What made our case unique was that we were not only highlighting that surely primary caregivers for children should have the same rights irrespective of their gender, we were also highlighting that there was an unconscious gender bias in place for us, as it took thirteen weeks to let us know that I was not entitled to enhanced pay and we were comparing our situation with the more favourable treatment that adoptive parents receive at The Authority. Just a reminder, our case is fundamentally different to the previously mentioned Ali case because we use the additional comparator of parents accessing adoption leave.

The following paragraphs are very, very dry but necessary to display how difficult the Employment Tribunal process is for a layperson to follow. It is taken from the Written Reasons by the Judge, as to why she went the way she did in her judgement:

'We reminded ourselves that the appropriate and correct comparator for the purposes of s13 and s23 EqA 2010, was a question of fact and degree and that all characteristics do not have to be precisely the same; just that they must not be materially different if one is to compare for like for like.

Mr Price has invited us to find that a female worker on adoption leave is an appropriate comparator as a male worker on shared parental leave as:

a. they do not have to undergo childbirth or have the trauma of childbirth;

b. He invites us to find that their role is on a par with a worker on shared parental leave;

c. He additionally argues that he has been with the birth mother from the outset of her pregnancy which places him in a closer personal relationship with the child as a result, than an adoptive parent would have with a child being placed with them.

'The Barrister on behalf of the respondent argues that the circumstances of a worker on Shared Parental Leave is materially different to a female worker on adoption leave for a number of reasons. Although he does accept Ali does not deal with any comparators other than a female worker on maternity leave, he invites us to find that a female worker on adoption leave is materially different to the claimant for the following reasons:

a. Adoption leave can commence before formal adoption leave (Paternity and Adoption Leave Regulations 2002");

b. The adopter does not need the agreement or consent of the other adopter to take adoption leave;

c. Adoption leave is acquired through the fact of adoption;

d. It can be taken at an age before maturity of the adopted child.

e. Shared Parental Leave cannot begin before two weeks after the birth date or, in the case of adoption leave, could not commence until the end of the compulsory adoption leave (as prescribed by Regulation 10(2) of the Maternity and Adoption Leave (Curtailment of Statutory Rights to Leave) Regulations 2014 ("Curtailment Regulations ");

f. Shared Parental Leave could be taken up to fifty-two weeks after this period and it can be 'dipped in and out'.

g. Shared Parental Leave can only be taken with a partner's agreement. It is acquired as a result of the adoptive parent giving up the statutory adoptive leave.

'The Barrister has also invited us to distinguish the purpose of adoption leave compared to the purpose of shared parental leave, and invited us to find that the adopter who has availed themselves and chosen to take the **statutory adoption leave has to deal with third parties as part of that adoption process, whereas the worker on shared parental leave is not necessarily so burdened.**

*Written Reasons extract and dryness over. *

    I have highlighted certain sections in bold to highlight why the judge's verdict and the barrister's reasoning was flawed in our humble opinion.

Forgive my Inspector Columbo impression here but 'There's one more thing' regarding the written reasons:

    '18. This definition is contained in the Glossary of Terms at the outset of the Shared Parental Policy. This also stated that "some employers will offer enhanced shared parental pay". This caused some confusion for the claimant, but it is clear from the reading of the policy, that the respondent did not offer enhanced shared parental pay.'

    I firmly believe that The Authority are misleading,

oppositional, and confusing by consistently standing behind their narrative that they are legally handcuffed from offering enhanced pay. They were (and continue with this stance in a statement in 2020) of the opinion that they were prohibited from legally offering enhanced Shared Parental Leave pay under the Shared Parental Leave policy. It is difficult to see that if they are aware that their stance is inaccurate given that the Welsh Government and National Health Service would not be able to offer its employees enhanced pay on Shared Parental Leave if they were legally handcuffed by the Shared Parental Leave policy too. The fact that they both decided to offer enhanced pay, and more to the point did at the time of the Employment Tribunal, continues to 'cause some confusion for the claimant'.

Unfortunately, the legal biz is underpinned by bucks. Big bucks and not justice. I justify this by barrister's salaries, allegedly charging upwards of a reported £400 an hour in my case. Even more so in more high profile cases. If this was all about the purity of justice, barristers would be doing this for far less money. It is a no brainer why legal eagles harbour a tight grip on the purse strings and refuse to relinquish any aspect of their precious jargonised, controlling, and ancient ways. As long as they can still charge £150 per letter rather than a free email, Skype, or telephone call, justice comes secondary to the good old pound and what is the incentive to reform and modernise.

On reflection, if a precedent was set and a blanket was thrown over every possible type of parent and all were entitled to share their primary caregiving role as their individual family remit dictates, then there would be thousands of billable hours lost to solicitors and the judges etc who rely on these individual challenges to make their money. It could be argued that it is not in the legal profession's best interest to set this precedent. Sounds pessimistic, but is clearly founded on some common sense.

What blows my mind to this day is how backwards the attitudes are within the British justice system. Their archaic ways are screaming out to be challenged. The fact that they have legally decided that a birth-mum is the nurturer, should be put up on a pedestal, and should have enhanced pay to the detriment of the validity of a biological father or any other type of parent is not in keeping with contemporary attitudes. Legally a birth mum can return to her professional role two weeks after giving birth, four weeks if they are a factory worker. If this decision is made it blows my mind even further that a primary carer is not entitled to the enhanced pay that the birth mum would have been entitled to if she had not returned to work.

Furthermore, there are currently forty-two recognised labels of how people wish to be identified as, that I have come across. Undoubtedly there are more that I have yet to come across.

Why wouldn't a judge representing British Law take a progressive Shared Parental Leave reform chance when the court system could be flooded with lucrative legal challenges, from any of the aforementioned identities who view they are as nurturing as any heterosexual mother is? All aboard the gravy train.

During the deliberation of my case, when comparators were discussed, it was evident that they are wide open for a field day of institutional discrimination challenges on the basis of identity equality on the basis of focusing on a gendered society. By the Court of Appeal deciding that birth mums deserve enhanced pay because they must breastfeed and are the most vital nurturing figure who has a greater need to bond with their baby than their partner, how does that make someone who identifies as feminine-of-centre/masculine-of centre feel?

It is a social minefield and a legal goldmine for the justice system.

Being transgender in a gendered society must be so demoralising when a birth mum is seen as the nurturer. Surely, that is a lasting vision of a bygone era. Surely, a progressive response to contemporary parenting is that a loving parent is the nurturer. A primary carer is the nurturer, irrespective of gender. Case in point, my wife wanted to return to part-time work after a few weeks, so why would my gender be a barrier to receiving the same enhanced pay that she would be entitled to, if I was stepping in as the primary carer? Where is the celebration of women's rights here?

This was my *Die Hard* finale, Hans Gruber moment. A myriad of loss. A smorgasbord of defeat, bitterness, disbelief, sadness, guilt, anxiety and utter failure. I had let down my daughter and wife, my extended family, friends, and all prospective parents who deserve equality. An epic balls-up! Case lost. Case closed. Bye-bye Justice. Bye-bye equality. Bye-bye progressive contemporary reform for all parents. Either you are part of the problem or you are part of the solution. Unfortunately the judge, her two silent assassins, and the barrister were members of Team Problem.

17
Noggin above the parapet

"Each time a man stands up for an ideal, or acts to improve the lot of others, or strikes out against injustice, he sends forth a tiny ripple of hope, and crossing each other from a million different centers of energy and daring those ripples build a current which can sweep down the mightiest walls of oppression and resistance."
   Robert F. Kennedy

I arrived home on the Friday evening after glumly driving home from Pontypridd Court, ruing my failure to even come close to achieving the ripple I intended to create. My pre-ET party line when discussing our challenge was, 'As long as we raise awareness and encourage a few people to have conversations on the flaws of the Shared Parental Leave policy, then that will be a success.' Well, in the fallout of trawling through the debris of our lost case over the next few days, I felt we had not raised enough awareness. We wanted to remedy this.

So, a few days later, on the Sunday afternoon we set up a Change.org petition. Neither my wife nor I had done anything like this before. I really want to send home the message that we are not an awkward couple with a history of enjoyment in being the thorn in anyone's side. We both believe strongly enough about our challenge that we were and are willing to risk our financial livelihood, my job, and all the additional collateral damage that has been part and parcel of this whole experience. This mostly involved, stress, sleepless nights, and anxiety. We looked at how we could best raise the issue with the elected army of seventy-three Powys County Councillors in order for the cabinet to put our grievance on their agenda. After all, they are the veins filled with the democratic blood of the taxpayers which feeds the entire LA machine. Seventy-three people who are not volunteers, I should add. Seventy-three people who after their salary, allowances, expenses, subsistence and travel, cost taxpayers £1,324,387 (2018-2019). Important folks to justify such an expense, I as a taxpayer would argue. We found an online article which indicated that if someone achieves fifteen hundred signatures on a petition regarding a council issue it will be discussed by the councillors. We found out a few days later that this was not a policy within Powys, but by this time our petition had garnered more momentum than a broken stair lift.

As the roles we tend to take in our relationship, I regurgitate my thoughts onto screen like a watering can's nose and my wife glances over it to make sure I have not been too cavalier with the nerve touching, reigning me in when necessary. Because we are decent people, we composed our petition blurb respectively and called it: 'Make parental leave provisions equal for all Powys County Council employees'

Here is a little taster of the blurb:

'I work as a youth justice worker for Powys County Council. Other parents working here, like mothers and those who have adopted, are given pay above the statutory minimum amount during their parental leave. So we assumed I could too.

'But instead I was told three weeks prior to our daughter's due date that I was not entitled to enhanced pay for my parental leave.

'This meant that as a father I couldn't afford to take time off, and missed out on spending time with my daughter during this incredibly important time in our lives.

'That's why I've started a petition asking for Powys County Council to ensure that all employees are offered the same enhanced benefits regardless of their gender.

'The reality of this policy really hit me one day while sitting between two colleagues. One was a father who could take time off with enhanced pay to bond with his son via the Adoption Leave policy - and rightly so. My female colleague had taken Maternity Leave on three occasions and also received enhanced pay to support her to take time off. This is exactly how it should be.

'But I, a biological father, was sitting in the middle and shared that I couldn't take time off to bond with my daughter beyond two weeks because I would not get the financial support that they did.

'In the year 2019 this is appalling and unfair. So I decided to launch a sex discrimination case against the council at an employment tribunal hearing. I had to represent myself against a legal department and barrister and was completely out of my depth.

'Frustratingly, we lost the case. But I won't stop fighting because I don't want other parents to go through the same. That's why I'm asking you to sign this petition so that Powys County Council will update their rules.'

In our opinions, the petition was clear, factually to the point, and did not celebrate the council's shortcomings or portray them in an unnecessarily negative light. What could go wrong?

We posted a link to our petition on our respective Facebook statuses and word spread like chlamydia during

Freshers' Week. It was obvious from the comment, shares, and likes that we were not the only ones who were surprised at the marginalisation of dads under the flawed Shared Parental Leave policy. Given that a few days earlier I felt like a chump for failing to get to grips with the council's Shared Parental Leave policy and this, and I quote, went on to 'cause some confusion for the claimant', it appeared that within my county I was not the only one who assumed wrongly.

Sass aside, we surpassed 1500 signatures in no time at all. Thank you, Mr Zuckerberg.

And then the sh*t well and truly hit the fan.

It was Monday morning, and I was back in the office. It was officially open season: 'There's a target on your back now', 'They'll take you out now for sure', 'Watch your back', 'Don't give them an excuse to sack you', 'Cover your arse'. These were just some super helpful reality-advice bombs being tossed towards me from my friends and colleagues.

Every day from here on in felt like a scene from *Hurt Locker*, with tentative steps on eggshells being the order of the day. The sword of Damocles dangled overhead and the inevitable impaling came with the delightful bedfellows of stress and anxiety. I knew I was doing the right thing and I knew the storm would disperse. Eventually. The question as to what debris would be left when it hit the fan, was anyone's guess.

If I introduced an app start-up company today, let's say a chicken poo tracker for the almost ten million resident chickens currently residing in mid-Wales, called 'FowlPlayers.com', and I told my new team of employees, 'Let's utilise this opportunity to make this app as brilliant as possible. Oh yeah, if any of you embarrass me by saying anything mean about me, you're sacked. Even if it's factually evidenced.' People would have every reason to question their human right of freedom of expression. And yet, at a local authority, its accepted as the norm. That just gives free reign to censor employees who are introducing a subject into a domain where taxpayers literally have ownership of their respective LA LA Lands.

18
Define 'Disrepute'

"He's not the Messiah—he's a very naughty boy!"
Monty Python's Life of Brian.

The word 'disrepute' is defined as: 'If something is brought into disrepute or falls into disrepute, it loses its good reputation, because it is connected with activities that people do not approve of.'

In order to put my repeated and valued notion of 'clarity and openness' philosophy into practice, and in order to resolve this issue without allowing the wider community to be aware of my employers' failings, I contacted ACAS off our own back after we felt unsatisfied by the council's response in July 2018 in order to openly and collaboratively raise our grievance in a professional and progressive forum. My employers fell at the first hurdle and failed to comply. In all honesty, it was a spectacular failure as our ACAS conciliator could not even manage to get a meaningful discussion with them. Off my own back, on the 23rd May 2019 I emailed the Chief Executive of Powys County Council, to share that there was an Employment Tribunal Hearing set for September. As I shared within the email, I wanted to be open and give her a heads up as to the potential negative fallout in the press following the hearing. I received a genuinely warm reply, which I was grateful for. I also emailed all seventy-three county councillors (well over a million pounds per years' worth of elected champions of a progressive council) on the 15th of September 2019, sharing how we lost our case, and also shared a link to our petition for more information, so they would also be in the loop should there be a negative fallout in the press. So, overall my conscience was clear and I was satisfied that I had not acted slyly and that nobody could say that I have had an agenda to embarrass my employers. I had been up front and stoically maintained a tight-lipped, closed shop regarding publicly voicing our disappointments online or in the press. Mostly because I did not want to poke the sleepy bear, get sacked and jeopardise my means of financially supporting my family. Particularly when taking into account the censorship of the looming 'disrepute' axe.

When the damp squib that was the ET Hearing came and passed, the game changed a wee bit. Since the 'Brecon and Radnor Express' journalist attended both days of the hearing, all the information shared was now in their possession and was soon to be shared in the public domain via their publication. Their article took pride of place on page one, two, and our story had more column inches than any other I could recall in my memory. The scheize had hit the proverbial and my face was pebble-dashed to the extent that I was partially blinded!

It was obvious that we had taken the moral high ground by expressing ourselves appropriately and not attempting to embarrass or attack anyone personally. We are challenging the unconscious bias against biological fathers within the Shared Parental Leave policy and the limp tokenism of The Authority's publicised 'Council Values' and 'Equality and Diversity policy'. Our specific short-term goal was to raise the public's awareness of these failings and to encourage some conversations on the topic. Our long-term goal is to hopefully be an ingredient within a recipe for parental leave reform.

The game changer was the publicity which gathered some momentum from the first Pen-y-Fan summit of the local press of the aforementioned Brecon and Radnor Express and the Powys County Times. This, in our minds, achieved our initial goal by being the catalyst of potential conversations regarding the Shared Parental Leave policy and how it is interpreted by Powys County Council. Now that the information, our story that is, was well and truly in the public domain, the Facebook and Twitter shares and retweets of our story and our petition grew significant legs. This resulted in reaching the second summit of Snowden when we were interviewed for an article in EachOther. This is a company that shines a light on Human Rights violations and marginalised groups, with over 68,000 Likes on Facebook and 29.7k followers on Twitter. As you can imagine, the article was pro our challenge and potentially raised our conversation with a significantly larger pool of people than previously. Soon after we hit the Himalayas. A reporter from Sky News called me and we pre-arranged a potential home visit with us for an interview. Soon after, we had an article in the Daily Telegraph on a Saturday of all days. I had never bought one in thirty-seven years on planet Earth. My enthusiasm dwindled rapidly when I saw it was £2.80 and had more supplements than a homeopath. It was a behemoth. Half a tree's worth at least. A local reporter and genuinely nice guy Rob had become our unofficial journalist since we were promoted from the lower leagues (I say that respectfully) and had played a blinder elevating our story from my little rural town's newspaper to the upper echelons of the national press. We thought we had peaked with regards to our reach now.

But then, then came our Everest. BBC Breakfast got in touch and I was on standby to go to Salford to be interviewed on the big red sofa. It was then that there was a building story of a virus that had originated in China and was beginning to take hold in parts of Europe. Our story was bumped and there was no more dialogue with the Salford team. We weren't bitter, after all we had surpassed the public reach, we thought we were going to have, and some.

A few days of silence was broken by an email from BBC Wales who also wanted to interview us. We agreed and a few days later, we had a lovely journalist and an equally lovely camera-operator at our house. They spent the afternoon with us. They filmed myself and Eliza playing in her playhouse and Eliza tearing it up in our village on her trike, followed up with a direct interview with me and my wife Laura. We laid our concerns bare in a very honest and candid manner. We could have censored our comments, but that would have been hypocritical given that we were exercising our civil right to free speech. Does free speech actually exist any more? As a council employee the council's zero tolerance towards discrimination underpins our challenge but the oxymoron of 'disrepute' makes for a censorship minefield.

It was a substantially cathartic experience for me as I had been consumed by this campaign for almost a year and a half by now. The stress and anxiety had crept in and I had not realised to how great an extent until I felt the rush of vindication when there was a microphone boom, a video camera on a tripod, and a BBC reporter asking us questions. Finally, I felt that we had a window of opportunity to make my employers accountable and be the moral high fliers that they claim to be.

Can you guess what happened next? You've got it. Covid-

19 arrived with an unceremonious crash-landing and obliterated all of our norms. Our story was parked for the time being.

The Authority's smorgasbord of game playing over the previous nineteen months had come to a crossroad in our face-off. King me. We had made it across the draughts board unscathed. Or so we thought.

19
The Authority Flex

'If you believe you're right...stand up and fight for your place in the sun. If you believe you can do it, hang in for the whole 15 rounds because even if you don't win, you will have earned the respect of everyone in the fight, including yourself, and in that sense you will have prevailed.'
Erin Brockovich.

The Mexican stand-off.

Over my twelve-year tenure it has taken this grievance for me to realise the entrenched toxicity of PCC. It's been like having a toxic frenemy delicately administering a drip-feed of poison. My once positive and optimistic persona has gradually been ground down to conform to a suppressive and broken system. It has turned that happy go lucky twenty-five year old into a pessimistic thirty-seven year old who is sick and tired of the 'bureaucrazy' sludge.

The following depiction of how I was treated so dismally, in addition to the catalogue of calamity prior, was akin to a spoilt child throwing a snot-bubbled, crimson-faced tantrum, which only went to highlight the 'one rule for us' and the 'other rule for them' concerning council value accountability. With their examples of truth-stretching surpassing even the most exaggerated Tinder profile. In a hashtag, it was #Utterbollocks to the nth degree.

Now to a few more supportive words from my emotional sponsors, my lovely colleagues:

'Don't give THEM an excuse to sack you.'

'They will make your professional life hell in order to make you walk.'

And so on and so forth. I have said it before and I will say it again, I have been blessed with the most supportive colleagues and line manager that I could possibly have had throughout this whole casserole of clusterf*ckery. Which was extremely welcomed given that the elephant in the room was that pointy Sword of Damocles hanging above my head. Impending doom awaited.

Next stop, social media. As an employee at my place of work, if you share a view that is in any way different to the corporate narrative, you are in violation of The Authority's social media policy and will be hit with the disciplinary stick until you learn to toe-the-line or are terminated from your post. Said beatings are justified by the presence of a literal bureaucratic 'Tick Box' exercise. When we log on to The Authority's network, we have to read the Social Media policy once every God knows how many years, and tick a box before we are allowed to access our emails and database etc. Is this really the way a progressive, positive, professional, open and collaborative corporation should act? To all the free speakers out there, the aforementioned is more like a suppressive, authoritarian, soulless, censored, and negative corporation. We cannot even take a dump to escape the corporate narrative being rammed down our throats because there is a poster portraying a utopian moral dream stuck on the inside of the stall door at eye level. As if Derren Brown has been paid by the council to consult them on how to hypnotize and subliminally mould us into the desired roadmap narrative.

The Authority Flex, post-petition bomb, came in the form of tactically sending in a friendly-faced previous mentor whom I respected for an impromptu off the record chat behind closed doors. The following five points paint you a rather disappointing picture to add to my already inept collage of balls-ups by various upper management figures towards us to date. If you are annoyed already, please take five, have a brew and take some deep breaths. Here goes:

1) My senior manager (a previous line manager and mentor who I shall name Bilbo because I am cut from a different cloth than his kind and am not going to publicly shame him) popped his head around the office door and requested that I join him for an impromptu, off the record, private chat. Bilbo shared that the Director (who I will refer to as Magoo) and Head of Service (whom I shall refer to as Blair) were unhappy with me as a result of the petition. Bilbo then asked me three questions. Firstly, 'Will I take petition down?' Secondly, 'Would I apologise?' And thirdly, 'Was I prepared to lose my job over this?'

It is important to bear in mind here that as these conversations and meetings were happening, we had committed to appealing the ET's decision and were liaising with a legal firm to represent us. Not only was my human right to Freedom of Expression being censored but my right to legally challenge a decision which involves my protected characteristic of gender, sex discrimination, being suppressed. I had no idea I was employed by Guantanamo Bay County Council!

I made it unambiguously clear that I believed strongly about what I was doing, and I would not take the petition down, I would not apologise, and if it comes to it, I was willing to lose my job if it came to that.

I shared with Bilbo that I was shitting myself with regards to how I felt at the end of this conversation given the three questions, as I was the main financial provider for a thirteen-month old daughter and my wife.

2) Bilbo invited me to a second meeting by email. There was no agenda and during the meeting Bilbo took the minutes. I was grateful to have my union rep present for support and he acted mainly as a witness. I was asked the same three questions. Would I take the petition down? Would I apologise? Was I prepared to lose my job over this?

I was told by Bilbo, and I quote, 'You've made your point. Now it's time to wind your neck in.' He told me that he would feed back the meeting minutes to Magoo, the director, and to Blair, the Head of Service, and reminded me again as to how unhappy they were with me. Bilbo shared he would do his best to help and seemed genuine.

3) My union rep informed me that because of the petition I might have brought the council into disrepute (embarrassed them by telling the truth) and I could get the sack for putting up a petition online. This was not because of the body of the petition blurb or the point I was making. It was purely down to the fact I specifically named Powys County Council within the petition's title. Furthermore, even though I was mindful to avoid writing anything derogatory myself, we had provided a forum for others to do so with the accompanying comments section on the petition itself and on Facebook and Twitter.

4) Bilbo sent an email invite for a meeting with him and Human Resources in a venue a half an hour away from both of our usual work bases. HR were involved so I assumed that the heat was increasing. Again, no agenda was sent with the invite. Within the body of the email it stated that we want to find a

way of moving forward. The fact that a HR rep was also invited suggested it was of a disciplinary nature, according to my union rep.

I agreed to attend initially, despite sharing in the email correspondence that Thursday was the only day of the week where I balance childcare within my working day. After discussing my predicament with my union rep, I emailed Bilbo to rearrange and asked for a venue at our work base and for any other day bar Thursdays, for the childcare reasons mentioned. I also asked for my line manager (a legend who I will refer to as Atticus) to be party to the emails and to be invited to attend this meeting too, because he had detailed knowledge of my experience from supervisions and heart to heart chats.

5) Bilbo sent me a second invite to a rearranged meeting, again without an agenda, agreeing to a change of venue. Sounds like we are getting somewhere. Until... unfortunately the meeting was booked for a Thursday again. He also refused to allow my line manager to be in the email thread or to attend because he wanted to feed back down to him via the managerial chain of command. I respectfully insisted that I wanted the support of Atticus there and Bilbo forwarded me an attachment of a copied email from the HR rep, who was also invited, stating it would be 'overkill' for Atticus to attend as well as my union rep. I once again shared that Thursdays are difficult due to childcare arrangements and he insisted that I should attend as it would not take long.

It was at this point when I physically, emotionally, and mentally hit a big ole wall. Over the fifteen months of dealings with my employers, I had gone from an optimistic, excited first time dad-to-be, to a frayed and hyper-vigilant guy who was exhausted, could not sleep, had occasional palpitations, and was as drained as a watering can without a base. My two best mates took me out for an evening meal, and I was so on edge that when a random person dropped their cutlery on the floor, I almost jumped out of my skin and was close to tears. In thirty-six years with a clean bill of physical and mental health, I was at an unrecognisable point. I visited my GP and did not return to work for another fifteen weeks. For all of you who have never experienced crippling anxiety, I was once like you. I always thought my chipper, laid back, confident, optimistic outlook was an invincible, invisible protective cloak that would deflect anything. I would best describe my anxiety as a baby elephant sitting on my sternum which prevents my diaphragm reaching its full rise and my chest felt like I was having a prolonged bear hug from a sumo wrestler. Toss in the inability to calm my mind at bedtime and perpetual ruminating thoughts making the usual unbroken 'sleeping like a baby' shift into a state of eye-burning insomnia.

It turned out that this previous 'invincibility cloak' attitude of mine was egotistical bravado and I was in fact utterly stress retardant. I avoided stress like herpes, until that day in July 2018 when we decided to challenge our employers' Shared Parental Leave policy. No more, no less, no pound of flesh, just a policy challenge. In that moment I could no longer draw on thirty-six years of a happy-go-lucky character forged in generally positive life experiences any more. No more dodging, avoidance, distraction, or procrastinating. With my wife bearing the brunt of parental responsibilities due to the very policy we were challenging, we agreed that I would take the brunt of the policy challenge. I had to front up and meet the stress head on, with nowhere to hide and it was completely and ridiculously relentless.

One of the saddest things about this particular experience was that Bilbo was someone I thought I knew well. He was 'Mr Principle', the genuine article. Or so I assumed. As mentioned, he was a previous line-manager of mine before he was promoted and I looked up to him as being a man of honour and a man of his word. I trusted him implicitly and was stung as a result, yet again. See a theme here? This reinforced how much power, money, and being entrenched in a broken system's lack of morality and connection with the employees changes some people. It was like a scene from the film Invasion of the Body Snatchers! Personal morals must be left at the doormat before logging in to The Authority.

I understand that the following attempt to make sense of the aforementioned points regarding my side of the story was a version from my bias, blinkered personal perspective, and was very emotive. I perceived point one as being unprofessional as it was an off the record impromptu chat with just the two of us. The three questions were a threat when digested in tandem with the sharing of my director and head of service being unhappy with me. I felt that I was being blackmailed and bullied to remove the petition and drop the case.

In point two I was asked the same three questions which sustained the threat of the first meeting. There was no agenda with the invite and despite my union rep being present, the minutes were taken by my senior manager. This allowed a biased account to potentially be recorded and a third party would have been more open. Was this a disciplinary investigation?

In point three being told by my union rep that employees have been sacked for less completely undermines freedom of speech and the censorship of my factual experience.

In point four, for the third time there was no attached agenda which was the catalyst for anxieties around a possible outcome and left me in the dark in terms of any preparation. Initially suggesting an awkward destination away from all of our bases was a pain. It may well have been that it was impossible to find a meeting room in our building at the particular time required.

In point five, there was no agenda for the fourth time. When being told I needed to avoid Thursdays as a result of childcare issues and rearranging to another Thursday added to the awkwardness. Worst of all, when I requested my line manager's presence I was denied. In an organisation which boasts openness, progressiveness, being positive and collaborative, this all stank worse than an Intensive Poultry Unit.

Parking my own bias and speculation of my treatment, it is valuable to take a helicopter view of the situation and acknowledge the 'dos and don'ts' of grievance management by the experts ACAS. First up let's explore whistleblowing. This is debatable in my case because what I shared was in the public interest and was in the interests of the mental health of parents, who are not allowed to access the more comprehensive parental provisions that are present in other places of work. Specifically, the NHS and the Welsh Government. But, some may disagree that I qualify as a whistle-blower. For more clarity on what a whistle-blower is, take it away ACAS:

'What is a whistleblower?

'You're a whistleblower if you're a worker and you report certain types of wrongdoing. This will usually be something you've seen at work - though not always.

'The wrongdoing you disclose must be in the public interest. This means it must affect others, for example the general public.

'As a whistleblower you're protected by law – you should not be treated unfairly or lose your job because you "blow the whistle".

'You can raise your concern at any time about an incident that happened in the past, is happening now, or you believe will happen in the near future.'

Thanks, ACAS. As a worker who is a whistle-blower regarding the subject of sexual discrimination, my protected characteristic of gender, within my employment which is in the public's interest given Powys County Council employs around 6,000 folks in my community. I am protected by law and should not be treated unfairly. Hmm, personal blinkered bias aside clearly my employers have dropped the ball by putting excessive and prolonged pressure on me. Evidenced by them asking me, 'Are you willing to lose your job over this?' and the pattern of skulduggery across the aforementioned five points.

Now we pop back over to ACAS for their step-by-step guide on how employers should handle a 'Grievance, by an employee'. Again, the lack of clarity rears its ugly swede. Because of the lack of an agenda, the initial 'off the record' unplanned surprise chat, the meeting minutes being taken by the senior manager and my line manager not being allowed to be present, I still do not know to this day if I took part in a grievance process. Back in July 2018, when I officially put our grievance in writing, we did not experience the following at all. Without further ado, we are going back to ACAS for an idiot's guide to handling a grievance:

'The Grievance Meeting.

'When an employee raises a formal grievance, the employer

should arrange to hold a meeting within 5 working days ideally.

'The employer should allow employees enough time to prepare for the meeting.

'The employer can arrange for someone not involved in the grievance to:

Take notes at the meeting.

Act as a witness if necessary.

'To keep the procedure fair, the employer should:

Consider information or evidence from all sides

See if a similar grievance has happened before and aim to follow the same fair procedure

'Employers should keep a confidential record of:

The meeting

Evidence they've gathered

Any decisions or actions taken

'The employee:

Should do their best to attend the meeting on the date set

Can bring any evidence about the grievance (for example, relevant emails) to show and discuss at the meeting.

'The right to be accompanied:

'By law, any employee or worker can bring a relevant person ('companion') to a grievance meeting, if it's about a legal or contractual issue. This is known as "the right to be accompanied".

'The person must choose their companion from one of the following:

A colleague

A trade union representative

An official employed by a trade union.'

Thanks again ACAS. With the more recent examples (see five points) of a senior manager popping their head around the office door and asking, 'Can I have chat?', then subsequently walking through the building to find an empty room to have a behind closed doors, one-to-one 'off the record' chat, not only left me very vulnerable as to what I said, but I was unable to prepare for the meeting. I was given the impression that he would protect me and unfortunately, that was either an empty promise or a cavalier attempt to fire-fight. Either way I was left feeling completely vulnerable given the aforementioned three questions. Whatever the initial intentions of the ad-hoc meeting, I was left feeling like I had been visited by a smiling assassin. I am no manager, nor do I have any ambition to be one within my line of employment, but I know that procedures are established to keep everyone protected and accountable.

But hey, maybe these meetings were neither regarding a grievance or a reaction to whistleblowing. Without the agenda, more to the point, the 'Headed Title' of the agenda to indicate what the hell it was all about, I was left clueless. Hence the fuel to the speculation which ignited an anxiety as to uncertainty of potential outcomes. If the meetings were not about whistleblowing or grievance, I can only assume that perhaps they were 'disciplinary' of nature. Over to you ACAS.

'A disciplinary procedure is used by an employer to address an employee's conduct or performance. A grievance procedure is used to deal with a problem or complaint that an employee raises.

A disciplinary procedure is a formal way for an employer to deal with an employee's:

Unacceptable or improper behaviour ('misconduct')

Performance ('capability')

What counts as misconduct

Misconduct is when an employee's inappropriate behaviour or action breaks workplace rules.

Some misconduct examples include:

bullying

harassment

refusing to do work ('insubordination')

being absent without permission (some people call it absent without leave or 'AWOL')

But your workplace might have its own examples.

Step 2: Following a fair procedure

If the employer has considered trying to resolve the issue informally but feels they need to start a disciplinary procedure, they must tell the employee straight away.

This should be done in writing and should include:

sufficient information about the alleged misconduct or poor performance

possible consequences, for example a written warning

The employee should have this information in time to prepare for a disciplinary meeting.

The employer must make sure they follow a full and fair procedure throughout.

This is for the protection of the employee, the employer and their business.

The importance of following a fair procedure

The Acas Code of Practice on disciplinary and grievance procedures is the minimum a workplace must follow.

You might have your own code or policy with some differences that better suits your workplace.

Although the Acas Code is not the law, if a disciplinary case reaches an employment tribunal, judges will take into consideration whether the employer has followed the Acas Code in a fair way.

Looking after employees' wellbeing and mental health

Going through a disciplinary procedure can be very stressful, so it's important that employers consider the wellbeing and mental health of their employee.

Looking out for the employee's wellbeing and offering support can help prevent:

Absence

Mental health issues arising

Existing mental health issues getting worse

For example, as well as regular communication, the employer could arrange any meetings in a more private and comfortable location if this would help the employee.'

Thanks again for clearing up the expected procedures ACAS. Now, I am still utterly clueless as to what the whole treatment I experienced, as mentioned in my points one to five, was all about. I have to believe that it was not a completely sinister way of trying to crush me to the point of presenting unfit for work. One thing is for sure, no account was taken as to the strain this was putting onto my already burdened mental health. I have to believe that it was more of an 'Authority Flex' administered by a previously trusted manager that went badly wrong. I have to believe the latter or else I work at a very dark place indeed. With me, my family, friends and colleagues, The Authority's stock in morality sat at a very, very low ebb. Prioritising their brand value over their moral value and their responsibility to the welfare of their staff.

To an observer, the path of least logical resistance was to compare our purist, altruistic endeavour with the greasy sludgy spider web of a broken bureaucracy. Our openness, honesty and integrity versus the censored, spun, cold brand, detached from morals and entrenched in power, wielded to gag and hide the truth to dodge their accountability.

To be as genuine as possible, I get it. Les gros fromages who include senior management, leads, directors, heads, and the chief, that is. Most of the players on the 'Power

Cheeseboard' that I have known have retired early. Mortgage free and sailed off into their respective comfy sunsets. Why would a big cheese risk their postcard perfect plan by popping their heads up above the parapet when home free and galloping towards the final hurdle, with a pension payoff looming? Very few people would have the integrity and the minerals to make that altruistic call. With their one eye on a vintage convertible, or a plot of land in the surrounding area of Alicante, or a custom designed VW Campervan, a world cruise, a ticket for the Orient Express, or a Route 66 road trip. Why would they risk losing out on that final salary pension pay-out? They are nestled within the chocolatey walls of Willy Wonka's factory with a golden ticket in their mitts. It would be a heroic act of deep, blue heroism if they were to publicly make a stance. I have yet to see an example of such an act. But, I get it.

The trouble with an 'Authority Flex', including the way I way mishandled and the threat of being terminated Sarah Connor style for publicly whistleblowing, is that it leaves a sleazy, sticky residue of immoral gagging-orders and censorship, which permeates the very DNA of the council's culture. Censorship and gagging individuals are tried and tested pillars of every cult and tyrannical dictatorship that have ever formed. To continue with the 'It's our way or das autobahn' pomposity, while les gros fromages are allowed to ignore the very values that staff below them have to work and live by online 'or else', is the proverbial 'Kool-aid' of persuasion. Drink up or jog on.

By mishandling my grievance regarding my sex discrimination claim, in a cacophony of negligence to my wellbeing over two years, they could argue that technically they are not doing anything wrong bureaucratically. Truth be told, morally, they are not doing anything right by doubling down and sticking to their guns either. An immoral checkmate. A professional and accountable set-up would officially investigate my actions in an open and clear manner and commit to a due process before concluding if they have grounds to act upon any evidence they uncover. That is literally all they had to do.

20
Strategy or Calamity?

"Just 'cause you got the monkey off your back doesn't mean that the circus has left town."
George Carlin.

The hindsight evidenced that Powys County Council were in George Dubya Bush league. It seemed that each week, sometimes each day, they would drop the ball in some new and unbelievably clumsy and unexpected manner. Hence the lingering question, was this a strategy or a natural disaster? The jury is still out. Local bureaucracy seems to be its own worst enemy in terms of living up to its own much-celebrated values.

In fairness, there was a moment of sincerity (I think) in January 2019 when I was grateful to have a sit down meeting with the Legal Lead from Powys County Council. In all honesty, she was warm, welcoming, limited jargon, and most importantly, I was able to share my side of things. The first time in this whole mess where I was felt to feel, at the least, a valued employee with a legitimate grievance. For that, I am grateful. In hindsight, I was asked 'hypothetically' what do I want to gain and was told that even if I win, the potential financial remedy would not be that substantial. I reassured her that this grievance was not motivated by financial gain and that is where that conversation died. Given what I know now concerning how much money has been thrown at gagging orders in recent years, I wonder where that conversation would have gone if my motivations were less righteously motivated.

The following paragraphs sadly put all of their previous tomfoolery in the shade. In the days running up to the ET Hearing they cranked their form up to eleven.

. As a frame of reference, the Employment Tribunal is explained within the Citizens Advice website as:

'Employment tribunals make decisions about employment disputes. Nearly all legal cases about employment are heard in employment tribunals. This includes cases about things like unfair dismissal, redundancy, and discrimination.

'In most cases, you must contact ACAS (the Advisory, Conciliation and Arbitration Service) to start early conciliation before you can make a claim to an employment tribunal.'

Having tried and failed to encourage an early negotiation via ACAS and to attain some expert or legal support, I achieved a series of mini-victories by meeting all but one deadline. The one I missed was an email address mistake which was remedied the following day. I felt victorious as I was as unqualified to take on my employer's legal department and barrister as a lame donkey in a quarter mile muscle car drag race. I had made each of the dozens of deadline hurdles, despite juggling the claim with my family life, a full-time job and maintaining my physical and mental health. Their efforts quickly became ridiculous. They were very consistent. Very consistent indeed. Very consistent at missing deadlines and dragging the whole experience out like it was always a perpetual afterthought.

I wonder how I would have been treated, if I had been as inefficient? Would I have been given the same leniency? As an opinion of someone who has been through the process, perhaps the ET would benefit from supporting claimants who represent themselves far more effectively by coaching them and at the very least, checking in to see how they were feeling, and if they were fully understanding the process. In all honesty, just any human support of any kind would have been nice. Perhaps a few face-to-face meetings along the way to share some clarity and guidance. After all, it would benefit them and the efficiency of the process too.

Out of interest and in the ole 'calamity or strategy' debate, I have explored the principles within the book *Art of War*. The work, roughly fifth century BC, is attributed to the ancient Chinese military strategist Sun Tzu. I fear I have been extremely negative and waxed lyrically and smugly about the potential ineptitude of leadership, so it is only fair to explore if there is any gravitas present for strategy. The thirteen chapters of *Art of War* are as follows:

1) Laying Plans.

Explores the five fundamental factors – The Way, Seasons, Terrain, Leadership, and Management. By thinking, assessing and comparing these points, a commander can calculate his chances of victory.

2) Waging War.

Explains how to understand the economy of warfare and how success requires winning decisive engagements quickly. This section advises that successful military campaigns require limiting the cost of competition and conflict....

It was at this point when I realised, I had significantly overshot the skillset of a local authority's strategic capabilities and prowess. I found it fairer and far more likely to compare the manner in which they have carried themselves with the novelties of an insurance broker's playbook, titled 'Delay, Deny, Defend.'

I was the lame young-ish lone wolf to their wolf pack. They had the elements of sharing the tasks amongst the pack with their increased numbers, surprise, they were not emotionally invested, and they had funds for a barrister at their disposal within their arsenal. I had the element of transparency, which ironically played into their hands given that I was challenging their own corporate values and sent them my List of Documents nine months before they sent me theirs.

So, here's the pickle. Can I attribute their conduct to the Peter Principle? The Ringelmann Effect? Or has the upper management 'Teflon Culture' (other non-stick brands are available) of avoiding accountability via such methods as being paid off, given gardening leave, or side-stepping into a different employment role, like a toddler playing hide-n-seek by placing their hands over their own eyes to make believe they are invisible? Or, is there a darker more sinister gameplay at foot? Or, does the former feed the latter like an all you can eat buffet? Who knows? One thing I can attest to in my twelve years as an employee here, is how the council's repetitive nature of dancing the same sorry dance and occasionally changing the tune to distract us plebs is just like Ouroboros. The what? It is the image of a serpent eating its own tale in an eternal recurring regeneration of life, death, and rebirth. Like the Hotel California, 'You can check out any time you like, but you can never leave!' That is to say, the present culture is trapped within the council like a genie in a lamp. Given the rurality of Powys and the fact that the council has the monopoly on employment, there is an element of feeling trapped. I studied a degree in Crime, Deviance and Society, hence my interest in youth justice and my employment within the council. If I was to 'check-out', I would either have to make a considerable commute, taking me away from what is important to me, time with my family. Or it would involve retraining or moving out of California altogether! Based on all the question marks it is clear that I do not have the answer.

My mentor in work, Johnny G, an absolute combination of Yoda, Sid James *(Carry on Films)* and the Godfather, guided me for my entire career to date and has recently retired. At pride of place on his notice board was a printed-off saying which read, 'We trained hard, but it seemed that every time we were beginning to form up into teams we would be reorganized. Presumably the plans for our employment were being changed. I was to learn later in life that, perhaps because we are so good at organizing, we tend as a nation to meet any new situation by reorganizing; and a wonderful method it can be for creating the illusion of progress while producing confusion, inefficiency and demoralization.'

Still, reigning back into the unacceptable behaviours I have experienced, I felt I was underselling their seeming skulduggerous nature and quite frankly had been a bit harsh on the insurance brokers' playbook. It was then when a more apt comparison came to my attention.

Come on in Mr Donald Trump with his 'Donaldisms'. Let me introduce you to his reported ten Ds of leadership. Before I proceed, I would like it made clear that in order to implement any of these 'Ds' as a strategy rather than embracing a moral code of conduct based on respect, the perpetrator has to be a massive 'D'. Trump's Ten Ds of oppositional tactics are as follows:

1) Deny, 2) Discredit, 3) Discount, 4) Deflect, 5) Delay, 6) Deceive, 7) Divide, 8) Dulcify, 9) Destroy and 10) Deal. Not forgetting the bonus D for discrimination.

1) DENY

The thirteen weeks wait for confirmation on what my entitlements would be came with the party line that the responsibility was solely down to the 'human error' of an individual administrative employee, as stated at the Employment Tribunal. Despite employment services, human resources and pay roll having a management structure where line managers are in place to supervise their employees and the senior managers and leads are paid substantial salaries to oversee and lead, ultimately, they could not possibly be held accountable. Despite the blanket, human apologies of the services involved which we received in the fallout of the mistake at the time. Quite the polar shift. Furthermore, because I responded with a grateful email at the time the barrister's, God love him, opening line of questioning during my cross-examination was that by me replying with said 'grateful email', I had surrendered any right to pursue a grievance.

2) DISCREDIT

Concerning Donald, it's fake news o'clock twenty-four-seven if anyone has a view opposing the big guy. Re-enter the barrister from the Employment Tribunal Hearing. When responding to my disappointment at the absence of gender equality he kindly added, 'We don't live in a perfect world, Mr Price.' During the UK Court of Appeal case a frustrating comment was made by one of the three judges in Ali and Hextall from 2019. She suggested that a dad could get a second job to bump up his wages if he is accessing a statutory pay based Shared Parental Leave. If such a suggestion was made about a mum there would be hell to pay.

My employers discredited us by failing to offer options to further pursue an independent ear and most frustratingly of all, they failed to meet with our ACAS conciliator.

3) DISCOUNT

Given the grey area of the Shared Parental Leave policy stating that 'Some employers will offer enhanced pay' the repeated rhetoric from my employers' spokesperson was that they could not offer any enhanced pay until the law was changed at a national level. I have shared until the cows come home that within Wales the National Health Service and the Welsh Government itself were and are offering enhanced pay. My employers stuck to their guns and maintained their stance, which opposed the 'Progressive' value published within their Council Values. Their party line echoing Donald here with 'We are not legally obliged to do anything.' See previous 'We don't live in a perfect world, Mr Price' comment.

4) DEFLECT

By putting the blame elsewhere and/or scapegoating someone. I refer to the 'Spokesperson statement' and the 'Human error' statements.

5) DELAY

It is alleged that Don welcomes endless delays by exerting executive privilege over documents and testimony. This sentence is eerily familiar with our experience. We had the initial thirteen-week delay, the month where they failed to have a meaningful conversation with ACAS, the three-week delay to my Notice of Hearing confirmation email which led to the ET hearing being delayed for ten months. I met my Witness Statement deadline of July 22nd and they sent theirs on July 30th. In addition, their most notorious Donaldism was their introduction of a second witness on the eve of the ET hearing. The icing on the cake being that I did not have the final Joint Bundle in my hand until an hour before the ET hearing when their barrister handed it to me. The icing on the icing of the cake being the 'Bundle Bungle' most heinously including the omission of key documents to my claim. All the delays! The Employment Tribunal itself agreed on September the 5th to send me the Written Reasons of our case in a 'few weeks'. I had to chase this up and received them on October 25th 2019.

6) DECEIVE

Deception is a clear sign of consciousness of guilt. The most effective lies always contain a kernel of truth. I would like to direct you to the spokesperson narrative; the Bundle Bungle; avoidance of implementing their own written values of being progressive, positive and collaborative; evading their responsibility to adhere to the Equality and Diversity policy and human rights.

7) DIVIDE

Trump appeared to divide the jury of public opinion with claims of fake news. The barrister, without precedent evidence discussed with the judge how elected Adoption Leave parents are entitled to enhanced pay on the basis that there are usually complications involved, which are not the case with my comparator of a dad on Shared Parental Leave. What the right honourable gentleman failed to add, in the spirit of proportionality and clarity, was that a family who adopt are allocated ongoing support via an allocated social worker from an Adoption Team. I am not. I also know adoptive parents who take exception to being tarred with such a brush.

8) DULCIFY

This was a new word to me. I have learned that Trump needs to do something good natured to give his supporters something to make him appear to be human. My employers don't legally have to pay enhanced pay for elective adoptive parents, but they do it any way out of the goodness of their hearts. As if this should be celebrated as them going over and above. In my humble opinion, enhanced pay for all parental leave pay should be a prerequisite as they are a body who employs thousands of people and is responsible for their welfare. The celebration of Council Values and their Equality and Diversity policy on paper should be the bare minimum of what and whom they are responsible for.

9) DESTROY

Don't like the message, denigrate the messenger and anyone who listens to them. What is disrepute? Censorship and threat of a disciplinary or termination.

10) DEAL

See later chapters…

(The Ten D's comparison was inspired by The Mercury News. Letter to the Editor. November 21st, 2018, at 9:06 a.m.)

Knowing I was a tone-deaf one-man band and prolonging the stress and anxiety with delay after delay, after delay, after delay, after delay, after delay. At the least, no consideration was given to my wellbeing. At worst, it was a chosen strategy in an attempt to get rid of me. I was being grinded down and all signs on my map were pointing towards a cul-de-sac known as 'A Fool's Errand.'

This has never been an attempt to embarrass and shame the council for a personal vendetta without a justifiable reason. It's about encouraging change through awareness. There is so much potential within the employee ground level and second floor. Unfortunately, the folks in the attic are haemorrhaging employee talent, the potential of a progressive and innovative culture, and public taxpayers' money. The roof is leaking on our house and sooner or later it will collapse on the floors below. I detest the current narrative and want the conversation to change for the sake of our future community. A community where I feel pride in displaying my employee ID badge when I'm out and about and I am no longer tucking my lanyard into my shirt out of embarrassment. Accountability and a commitment to change with regards to gender equality within their Shared Parental Leave provisions would be a great 'baby step'.

If one was to be so bold as to play the role of devil's advocate (obviously I cannot play said role as I am an employee and would therefore jeopardise my career), then they might make a comparison between the aforementioned senior managers and upper echelon leader types, and the 'made men' in the mob. There is an aura of untouchability around them. The presence of golden handshakes, gardening leave, being paid out of their contracts for failure, are all available to them and not to the foot soldiers below them. Not just different rules, but a different sport altogether.

The mob families were managed by the boss, the under-boss, and several captains. Their version of 'council values' was 'the code'. Any breaches of this code would inevitably end up with a baseball bat to the patella, a severed racehorse's head in your bed, getting whacked and sleeping with the fishes. Running the show under the illusion of it being run legitimately by a democratic rule via elected union men.

'Ringing any bells?' a devil's advocate may ask. See £400,000 spent on gagging orders (non-disclosure agreements with departing staff) between 2018 and 2020, and £4 million spent on one hundred and fifty such arrangements between 2005 and 2019, and the knee-capping censorship control of the 'Bringing the Council into Disrepute Enforcer' via the social media policy.

In order to run a successful mob family, you must rule with an element of fear. The devil's advocate, the rascal, may say that the prospect of job loss is the council's element of fear. With electricity and heating bills, mortgages, food, fuel, debt etc., most of us are only a few pay days away from being crippled financially. Censor masters of our freedom of expression and moral launderers. Toe the line in public and in your professional role by keeping shtum about the employer's failings or face the 'Disrepute Enforcer.'

The devil's advocate may say that over and over and over again the council show just how little respect they have for the elected councillors and how they appear to actively diminish the voices of the employees and the taxpaying public, by continuing along on their own self-architected road map, which is devoid of any true accountability and public scrutiny. Any change will only ever truly and legitimately occur with an overall institutional reform, starting at the top and cascading down to the foot soldiers. Rather than the tired, tried and tested and failed bottom-to-top trend. The place for shady, behind closed doors, censored gagging orders and payoffs for mistakes should be a sign of just how much their fundamental structural reform is required. There is an obvious lack of confidence in the council by the electorate as the council have an entrenched brand of being detached and unaccountable for the decisions made with the taxpayer's money. Some might say the whole establishment is a fugazi. Forget about it!

Case in point, Abermule is a small rural village in Powys. Two hundred villagers turned up at the council HQ to protest against the cabinet's overrule of the councillors' vote to refuse the planning of an industrial bulk recycling plant adjacent to the village. Local Authority democracy in practice some would say. Did that make a difference? Nope. No siree. If there was one man and his dog and his placard rocking up to protest, it could be argued that his view is not representative of the whole of Abermule and surrounding area. But two hundred protesters? This could only result in the expansion of the chasm between The Authority and Powys residents. Residents who, by the way, are footing the bill for the decision makers' salaries. Odd, very odd. Forget about it!

The councillors' roles should be more than a rubber-stamping exercise for whatever The Authority wants to do. Councillors and taxpayers should not only be consulted, but the council's proposals should be scrutinised and democratically decided upon by the taxpaying public via their elected representatives. A council cabinet should not be allowed to overrule the elected councillor's votes. The Authority's upper echelon and cabinet must be held accountable in a completely open and accessible manner.

Another case in point, the pal-y pal-y nature of the agricultural industry's influence to allow one hundred and thirty completed applications for Intensive Poultry Units in Powys between 2015 and July 2020, with twenty-nine more in the pipeline. A council spokesperson stating that they are 'powerless' to agree a taxpaying group's request to sensibly hold a moratorium to pump the brakes and scientifically explore the potential environmental implications. (A narrative all too familiar with our campaign as a spokesperson shared their hands are tied until the government acts to force them to pay the enhanced pay. Despite there being a moral option already written into policy to do so.) This raises the questions of, who does have the power? Who is in charge of allowing a gold-rush style approach to ensuring that Powys continues to reign supreme as Europe's capital of intensive poultry units? Is it the poultry industry itself? The supermarkets? Agro-farming industry? Welsh Government? A devil's advocate may leave you with this little detail. An intensive poultry development which houses over 85,000 birds falls under Schedule One of the Town and Country Planning (Environmental Impact Assessment) Regulations 2011, the same category as a new airport or a nuclear power plant (Information sourced from the Campaign to Protect Rural England website). In the summer of 2020, Powys was rapidly approaching ten million chickens. Forty-five million if you include Shropshire's and Herefordshire's IPUs. It doesn't take Homer J Simpson to recognise that we are blindly racing between post-Brexit world and an environmental meltdown! Never mind eh. There will be no way they can threaten anyone to 'sleep with the fishes!' because there will be no fishes left in our rivers as a result.

21
Cap in Hand

"After all, one can't complain. I have my friends."
Eeyore (Winnie the Pooh - A.A. Milne)

After much deliberation between the members of Team Price after receiving advice from our barrister's merits assessment, we decided to make a substantial investment in a fifty/fifty chance of achieving accountability and justice. We felt and thought that personal financial burden, the likelihood of stress, anxiety, risking my job and future career progression were worth the risk of losing at the Employment Appeal Tribunal. What we were most worried about was the worst possible outcome of my employers retracting their provision of enhanced pay for parents who access Adoption Leave. This was something that our barrister pointed out as a potential outcome should we wish to pursue our case at the EAT.

The thought of going hell for leather with the intention of nudging my employers to accept their corporate responsibility for equality and the outcome being a regressive retraction of enhanced pay for adoptive parents, on the basis that we used them as a comparator who are treated more favourably, would be an absolute disaster in our view. We decided to go for it, for the greater good and because it was morally the right thing to do. In our humble opinions.

'They couldn't and wouldn't be that callous as to pull adoptive parents' enhanced pay!' we heard many of our friends and family say. Well, the following paragraph of just how dastardly they can be may sway you towards why we were so worried.

Serendipity can be a cruel mistress. As you have been well versed by now, three weeks before our first baby we were told about there being no enhanced pay. Three weeks before our second child was due (during lockdown in a pandemic) we were informed that our twenty-year-old, consistently successful work team which continually reduced youth crime, had extremely low staff turnover, high morale, and extremely low sickness levels, was being restructured. Just to add some human context. At the start of the Covid-19 pandemic, projections estimated that up to fifty percent of frontline children's services staff could be off with the virus. We, as a team, were asked to help. We all got on board no questions asked because you do not go into our line of work without the desire to help others. Out of our team of twenty, approximately seventy percent of us were redeployed into the various tentacles of children's services. Despite the trajectory of staff absence being completely wrong and a non-entity, thankfully, we were not allowed to return to our original teams. Especially odd given that there was a mini youth crimewave and our service was arguably busier than ever. In addition, five of our team members were now off with stress. In my twelve years I have never know more than one person to be off with stress. Then it all became very, very clear. Our senior manager, a once seemingly principled bloke (you will be familiar with his work from the previous chapter) shared an email with us which he asked to be forwarded to us via a senior member of our team.

Bilbo then went on leave for a week, leaving us to fester in anxiety. The email shared that our team was in the process of being permanently restructured. It appeared that in his cold opinion, and (more to the point) the opinion of the head 'Blair' and director 'Magoo' of Children's Services, it was the right time, during a pandemic, to share that not only is our team being dismantled, and potentially being pimped out to help the sinking HMS Children's Service, but there is a likelihood of redundancies for some of us. During a pandemic. An awful example of how power distances people in a hierarchy. Particularly disgusting during a pandemic and in such a stealth opportunistic manner. Cold, callous and horrid. Ten days after his return to work he sat in our team Skype meeting. When asked by an upset staff member about rolling this plan out during a pandemic, with an unprecedentedly high caseload and under the sly guise of us being asked to voluntarily redeploy into teams to cover the absence of Children's Services staff, as a result of contracting the coronavirus, he replied with a shrug and shared there is never a good time for a restructure. Upper echelon Powys County Council at its most callous anti Council Values behaviour. Prior to this job, back in the day, my understanding of a contract was to clarify my legal obligations and specific responsibilities to my post. After a job re-evaluation a few years back, I became aware of a caveat in my contract that states that as an employee I can be required to fulfil any other duty that is deemed reasonable by my employer. A 'get out clause' for the employer in laypersons' terms. We were under no illusions by now that we were completely outgunned.

My wife and I made our decision to continue upon this whacky journey and we were going for gold. Our solicitors and our barrister agreed kindly to cap our total fees at £5000. 'Kindly' I hear you gasp. Well, given that the barrister representing the council at the ET hearing was reportedly being paid in the region of £400 per hour, we counted ourselves extremely lucky. We hoped, in secret, the fact they were offering us a capped fee was because they saw a potential coup for them in being the main players in setting a new legal precedent. The wife and I are not renowned gamblers. The Grand National and the occasional Lucky Dip Lotto ticket when we feel fruity, but otherwise not. This was our uncharacteristic 'all on black' moment. We were throwing ourselves on the mercy and the goodness of others, and strangers at that.

It was a hail Mary, an all-in attempt to go for broke. It was our 'Skywalker Window'. Luke had a two-metre gap in the enormous Death Star to take it down with a proton torpedo in his iddy-biddy X-Wing. The Force was strong with him and he made it on behalf of the Rebel Alliance. We were hopeful that by enlisting the aid of the dark arts specialists alongside our 'Force', it gave us a new hope of discovering and shooting the Shared Parental Leave policy's Achilles heel, The Authority itself. By using their apparent unconscious bias, tokenistic policies and so called 'values' against them in a legal medium, we hoped that their greasiness would help lubricate the omnipotent cogs of justice and awaken the force of good, progressiveness, and righteousness.

Doubts? Of course, we had some.

Was our fight too soon? By chipping away, are we really going to make a significant difference? Was it worth prolonging our anxiety and stress with the addition of a petition and the crowd justice crowdfunding? How entrenched is the unconscious bias? How progressive are we trying to be in comparison to others? Do people actually care? I mean, really care? Or do the masses prefer to succumb to the warm, fuzzy glaze of distractions such as sport, reality TV, and social media? In fairness, I get the 'bubble reality.' That closing the house door when you get home, shutting your world in and the corresponding feeling of being 'happy with your lot' and impervious to the dark external forces. We are all consumed by time management and debating if we are spending enough quality time with our loved ones. After cooking, feeding, cleaning, laughing, entertaining, role-modelling, walking the dog, exercising, etc., is there enough room to be mindful and present if we continue? Sweet Jesus where's my beanbag? I need to lie down.

Serendipity played a vital role in the rest of our story. Post-petition online fallout, my sister-in-law was getting her boogie on at a local wedding and bumped into a lovely lady who found out that I was her brother-in-law and took an interest in what my petition was all about. A drunken screenshot of the friendly stranger's details arrived with myself shortly after with their contact details. The catalyst which gave our case the much-needed CPR was a tipsy dancefloor encounter.

On the following Monday I called the solicitor and there soon followed an introduction to a barrister with a stellar career and a specific set of skills in discrimination cases. He was our very own Bryan Mills (Liam Neeson's character from the film Taken). He undertook a Merits Assessment on our claim and came back with some good news and some very scary news. The former was that we had a 'fifty-fifty' chance of winning in his opinion. The latter was that he shared that the worst possible outcome could be that my employers withdraw their progressive provision of enhanced pay for an elected adoptive parent. Therefore, there was a potential reality where we could win the case and the outcome would be that not only would we be ineligible for enhanced pay on the Shared Parental Leave policy, but adoptive parents could be stripped of their provisions which were on par with the Maternity Leave policy provisions. In short, we could play a key role in pushing the Local Authority away from our desired destination of progressive equality for primary care givers of all genders. It was a sobering thought.

After much deliberation my wife and I mutually concluded that it was time to get off the pot and attempt to flush away the bureaucratic fugazi that is The Authority's 'Council Values' and 'Equality and Diversity policy.' I had poked the bear and it was pissed off. Now was the time to run my sword of justice through its dark heart as it attempted to maul me.

22
All aboard the Appeal Train!

"Let me tell you something you already know. The world ain't all sunshine and rainbows. It's a very mean and nasty place and I don't care how tough you are it will beat you to your knees and keep you there permanently if you let it. You, me, or nobody is gonna hit as hard as life. But it ain't about how hard ya hit. It's about how hard you can get hit and keep moving forward. How much you can take and keep moving forward. That's how winning is done!"
Sylvester Stallone, Rocky Balboa.

After much deliberation between the members of Team Price after receiving advice from our barrister's merits assessment, we decided to make the substantial investment in the aforementioned fifty/fifty chance of achieving accountability and fingers crossed, some positive changes. We felt and thought that a personal financial burden, the likelihood of stress, anxiety, financial burden, risking my job and future career progression were worth the risk of losing at the Employment Appeal Tribunal.

We gave the green light to our solicitors and barrister. On the 3rd of December 2019, our legal representatives submitted our appeal. Now it was a waiting game. By now, we were in our second year of our waiting game and becoming quite adept at it. We were informed that our submission would be sat in what was called a 'sifting process', with the good folks of the Employment Appeal Tribunal and we just had to wait and see. Fast-forward to two thousand five hundred pounds (give or take) later, on the 5th of June 2020 I had an email from our lovely solicitor who confirmed that they had heard back from the EAT and a decision had been made. (Insert a cold, clammy brow, a dry throat, and an increased heart rate here.) It was at this moment that our journey could have arrived at its final destination at the far edge of the final page of our A-Z Roadmap. All rested on the following omnipotent email. For the sake of the pursuit of a just ending, our story continued as we were told that, 'Although the first ground of your appeal has been rejected (comparator of birth mums with biological dads) due to the fact that it was based on the Ali case which did not succeed before the Supreme Court, the remainder of your appeal (comparator of adoptive parents with biological dads) will be listed for a full hearing.'

To my limited understanding, there were only two potential outcomes to this news. My employers could 'settle' which we would hope would be a change in policy to offer enhanced pay from now on to my parent colleagues at the council who access it in the future. Or we would go to a full hearing at the Employment Appeal Tribunal and our claim could take another run at the respondents with a new and improved offensive team. Either way, we were still alive and kicking.

Regarding the next step, there was nothing that we needed to do except wait a further twenty-eight days for my employers to respond officially and legally confirm their position. Can you guess how this played out? By now, I am sure you can.

July the 2nd 2020 came. It was deadline day, again. Surely, this time it would be different. The twenty-eight days EAT appointed window had passed without so much of a peep to my solicitor or to me. In absolute fairness to my employers, we were now amidst the surreal and unprecedented era of Covid-19. Therefore, I could assume that any delay was down to the disruption relating directly with the effects of the pandemic. I would be more confident in saying that if we had not experienced the debacle of their previous actions over the past two years. I'll write that again for emphasis, two years. Two years of our lives where hundreds of hours were wasted if you consider that the right thing for them to do was right in front of their noses from the very beginning. Ever since the introduction of the Shared Parental Leave policy in 2015, if you want to be wholly accurate. When my mind wonders to the length of time it has taken, it makes me rue their lack of commitment to address this issue with ACAS at the very first hurdle in the summer of 2018. The mind continues to boggle.

Following the aforementioned 'Sword of Damocles' in the aftermath of our petition, I had now entered a very odd chapter of this whole process. The 'MAD' chapter. The chapter of Mutually Assured Destruction. If we had not pursued an appeal and indeed managed to gain legal representation, there could have been a target on my back for 'embarrassing' my employers with my 'disparaging and damaging' remarks. It would have been down to their discretion as to whether they themselves interpreted my petition as bringing them into disrepute. To paraphrase my union rep, 'people at this council have been sacked for less.' However, since the bullying and haphazard management of my dressing down from senior management, as mentioned in 'Authority Flex', if I was to get sacked I had, for want of a better expression, ammunition for an unfair dismissal. Furthermore, to discipline or sack me since my appeal became official would have been a public relations disaster for them and would have pushed this all into the dark territory of a potential constructive dismissal (me resigning as the result of my hostile working environment) or an unfair dismissal. I would not wish the constant threat of being disciplined and the aforementioned mishandling of myself on anyone. Sacking an employee who is pointing out failings of the employer, which are already in the public domain thanks to the press, in an honest and open manner could have led to dozens more column inches in an array of publications and could have led to a waste of taxpayers' money in a possible pay-out. The Cold War in mid Wales. From my perspective, if I threw my proverbial toys out of the pram and shared hateful and untrue thoughts online about my employers, they would be in a stronger position to terminate my contract and in doing so I could risk my EAT case. Hence the potential catch-22 merry-go-round.

It was a time of reduced anxieties for me as it felt as though I had bought some calm time and some breathing room where I felt as though I could be me again. The best version of myself returned and patiently awaited some closure, and we hoped it would arrive hand in hand with common sense.

23
Employment Appeal Tribunal Hearing Day-ja vu The Last Crusade!

"Insanity is doing the same thing over and over again and expecting different results."
   Albert Einstein (allegedly).

At the original first bout at the Employment Tribunal Hearing, I was just a guy standing in front of a girl, asking her to love parental equality. This time around at the Employment Appeal Tribunal Hearing, I was just a guy, sitting at my laptop behind a guy on a video gallery, who was asking a guy to see some common sense and overturn an archaic decision. This time around it felt less emotional, stressful, and personal, as we were confident that, this time, we had an arsenal of litigation weaponry fit for such an occasion. Step up to the plate our barrister supreme.

The surreal thing with being represented remotely during a plague with restrictions galore is that I never even spoke to our barrister, let alone met him. In comparison I had a very close relationship with my solicitors. One of which I know as a friend of a friend who is a lovely person called Sarah who for all intents and purposes seemed to oversee our case while her colleague was the hands-on contact for us. Brilliant people who were extremely supportive throughout. I was genuinely going to really miss my contact from my solicitors. It was on par with Stockholm Syndrome as they had been a consistent buoy of support and I was obedient to their decisions. I became an emotional hostage to my legal handlers. Even though my ransom came at a cost of £5k paid for by ourselves and our incredible consortium of 111 generous like-minded people.

The message that I failed to eloquently share at the original ET Hearing was that in comparison the Shared Parental Leave policy is 'The Elephant Man' at the prom of parental provisions. We are sat to the side of the gymnasium's dancefloor, alone and dribbly as the pretty adoptive parents and birth mums take pride of place in front of the DJ, dancing and having a great time at their prom.

Sat in my shirt at the kitchen table/home office workstation/dining table watching a weird version of Celebrity Squares or more like a Catchphrase bonus round. What's Mr Chips up to here? No idea, but we've raised £5000 to find out. Top left was our man. Top middle and top right had their initials and the middle row had the judge centre stage, flanked by two very deadpan deputies. I initially appeared in shot and saw that others were muted and turning off their video so I sputtered a 'Morning', before retreating to a voyeuristic stance of audio and video silence faster than an elected politician ditching their manifesto. I was appearing from the comforts of my own home, drinking tea from my own mug with my wife and six-month-old son sleeping in her arms as she in turn was watching the hearing on her laptop. Compared to September 6th, 2019, where I was suited and booted and as uncomfortable as a rabbit in an animal testing laboratory.

On January 26th, 2021, I was far from relaxed but a damn sight less anxious than back in Court Room Two of Pontypridd Court sat sweating in my wedding suit, naively hoping that justice would prevail regardless of my adversarial skills (or lack thereof) as the facts would speak for themselves. A harsh lesson I learned from that experience. Taking on an experienced barrister when you are an emotionally attached layperson is akin to a blindfolded, drunk child fighting against a reigning bare knuckle boxing traveller champion. If ever there was an example of someone being as close to absolute vulnerability, it was then. Which meant that today was likely to be a far calmer experience where any questions coming my way would be highly unlikely and the likelihood of it being another psychological dent would also be highly unlikely. There was a calmness present on this day. Derived from a reflection that my wife and I had taken this as far as we possibly could and regardless of the outcome, have made far more people aware of the flaws of the Shared Parental Leave policy. We were hoping to ignite a fire within the stupid policy and send smoke signals far and wide. Either to celebrate or to empower other regular folks like us to challenge it.

24
Judge Judy and Executioner

"Those who have the privilege to know, have the duty to act."
  Albert Einstein

DISCLAIMER - The following is based upon alleged information shared by my previous line manager, Atticus, on the morning of the Employment Appeal Tribunal Hearing at nine thirty a.m. The hearing's online sign-in was at ten fifteen a.m. and I was walking to the village shop to buy cookies and popcorn to settle down for the big show. As mentioned previously, on the eve of the September 2019 Employment Tribunal Hearing, my employers dropped a last-minute bomb by sharing that they were adding a surprise witness to proceedings. If you thought that was a curveball, you are not going to believe the following. All my suspicions, instincts, and paranoia were completely on point. Allegedly.

I never, ever wanted to be in the position of 'Judge Judy and executioner' but the sheer egotistical arrogance of the aforementioned Magoo, Blair, and Bilbo (the latter who I now really feel for as a result) pushed us as far as we could go.

Here is where the grease begins to settle on the surface. Potentially and speculatively I should add. As with the ET Hearing, the day before I emailed the Chief Executive, who by all accounts and to give them their dues has been a diamond, that there could well be some negative press to follow. In a small back and forth I shared that I am under the impression from the support I have had from my union rep and the line of questioning from my senior manager that there is a strong likelihood of being sacked for breaching the social media policy and bringing my employers' reputation into disrepute. They assured me that my job would not be affected for speaking openly and challenging a policy. I could literally feel that sumo wrestler bear hugging me loosen a tad and the baby elephant rolled off of my abdomen. Relief of the likes I have never experienced after believing for fifteen months that I would be sacked as soon as we had a verdict. Within three days of me sharing Bilbo's antics with the Chief Executive, he had resigned. Coincidence or corporate arse covering? Either way, Bilbo has strutted off into the sunset with his fat pension secured for an early retirement.

Now, here is where the corporate inconvenient truth-bomb is dropped from a great height and turned the greasy surface, left by Bilbo's departure, into an oil slick worthy of a Rainbow Warrior protest! By this point Atticus had left our pastures and been working outside Powys for around six months, and I really missed him as a mate and a manager. Prior to him leaving he shared that there was something he wanted to share with me one day when the timing was right. Bear in mind, there were occasions in the midst of all of Bilbo's shenanigans and on my return-to-work post stress-related sick leave where Atticus literally teared up when we discussed my case, or repeated that he felt guilty for not doing enough. Absolutely untrue as I know how much I appreciated his support back in those dark days. Fearing that he would regret not sharing his secret with me if it could potentially strengthen my case, Atticus decided to call me.

Atticus alleged (and was willing to make a statement if needed) that around the time Bilbo had threatened me with losing my job and told me to wind my neck in, he also told Atticus that if he didn't lean on me to drop my gripe, he could also be sacked! I felt sick when I heard this. The level of Machiavellian arrogance was crazy.

As a minion I have had the Council Values rammed down my throat more times than I can remember. It's lauded as a big ole disciplinary stick by which us employees have to work and live by or else. Now, that's all well and good if it is part of an all-encompassing dogma for every single council employee. Every single one. No exceptions.

I bounced between 'let sleeping dogs lie' to 'what if someone else is treated with similar intimidation in the future?' Either I live by the moral high ground I want to see everywhere, or I become an enabler. Harbouring a bully because I cannot be arsed to go through more boring, time consuming, stressful hoops again.

The overarching issue that Atticus and I deliberated on was that Bilbo was the spanner in the proverbial works. Bilbo was primed to be the fall guy. Every corporate battle needs a scapegoat and shit always rolls downhill. If (more than likely when) Blair and Magoo deny ever giving Bilbo the order which led to him reluctantly instructing Atticus with the words 'I know it's horrible, but we have no choice!', or if they were to say Bilbo misinterpreted them, then our claim would be dead in the water. Power and ego is everything one minute, and grains of sand running through fingers the next. The perfect storm of arrogance, megalomania, and having their ego challenged by employees from way, way down below their station could be just the tonic to wash some soap and water karma down their filthy throats.

To pump the brakes, indicate and turn into the entrance of Perspective Motel, it is pertinent to realise that the three amigos must have believed they were doing right by their team. As an avid believer that there is inherent goodness within us all, some is buried deeper than others it has to be said, I have to believe that my opinion of Bilbo, Magoo, and Blair is specifically based on my individual experience in a snapshot of time. Many grains of sand have fallen through the sand timer since then and many more will continue to do so until the upper half is empty. After all, there are always three sides to a story. Our side, their side, and the unbiased true version in the middle. We make decisions based upon the view and information we have at a given time and unfortunately for me and Atticus there were some odd calls made against us. I have to believe that when they are home with their feet up 'Netflix and chilling' or playing fetch with their dog etc., that their inner goodness is closer to the surface. This is all one big old learning curve and without rubbish decisions we can't grow.

25
The Verdict

Do not go gentle into that good night, Old age should burn and rave at close of day; Rage, rage against the dying of the light. Dylan Thomas.

Thank you for taking your precious time to hear our ridiculous tale of woe. Our post-verdict press release bow was as follows:

The past nine hundred and ninety-nine days have been like a perpetual Benny Hill Show sketch. With bemusing delays, very questionable behaviours, bizarre attempts of intimidation, blatant discrimination, and more hoops to jump through than a Crufts agility demonstration! I have buckled on a few occasions (would have been more if it wasn't for Laura's support) and wasted hundreds of hours on learning, preparing, presenting, and crowdfunding for what should have been a completely unnecessary case. To rub salt into the wounds, we have poured over £5000 of our own and supporters' money into this which has amounted to nothing.

The fact that in 2021 we have had to take our grievance all the way to the Employment Appeal Tribunal (EAT) to ask why a biological dad on Shared Parental Leave (SPL) is not entitled to enhanced pay on par with adoptive parents and biological mums, just goes to show the reality of parental gender inequality. At the core of our grievance is the frustration that employers have the power to decide whether or not they offer enhanced pay on the SPL policy. Some do, some don't.

Nine-hundred and ninety-nine days ago on July 23rd, 2018 – after waiting thirteen weeks to get our Shared Parental Leave request processed – we formally complained about the absence of enhanced pay for biological dads at Powys County Council (PCC), on the grounds that it reinforces the gender pay gap because of a lack of equal opportunities in the workplace, due to stereotypical parental role expectations, i.e. Male breadwinners and females staying at home to nurture the children.

Here's where the mind boggles. PCC present an annual report called the 'Mandatory Gender Pay Gap Report'. In 2017 it shared 'the Council believes in creating a diverse and gender balanced workforce.' In 2018, 'the Council is fully committed to closing the gender pay gap.' PCC's Gender Pay Action Plan 2019-2020 and 2020-2021 adds 'Ensure that PCC is an attractive place for all employees to work and appeals equally to all genders.' Vision 2025: PCC's Corporate Improvement Plan 2020-2025 (published March 2020) states that PCC is committed to 'Take action to close the gender pay gap. *One of our equality objectives.'

Based on these progressive statements, it's very odd that our policy challenge met any resistance whatsoever.

It has been an exhausting honour to have played the voluntary roles of 'equality accountability ambassadors' and supported PCC by attempting to steer them in a progressive direction of travel on their road map for Vision 2025. Perhaps we should pass the baton onto Specsavers.

Thank you to everyone who has signed our related

petition, the one hundred and thirty donations to our crowdfunding pot for legal representation, and for every share, positive comment, kind ear, cwtch (when that was allowed) and words of support. We will forever be grateful. A special thank you to our great solicitors and our incredible barrister. The latter's summary from our EAT Hearing is as follows:

'A recent survey has indicated that only 3% of fathers take their shared parental leave. The reason for this is likely to be that unlike their partners, they do not receive their full pay for some or all of the period. In Price v Powys County Council (UKEAT/0133/20), a case where I represented the Appellant, the EAT rules that man who proposed to take shared parental leave was not entitled to compare himself to a woman on adoption leave who, under the Council's policy, was entitled to receive the same enhanced payments as a woman on maternity leave. The EAT ruled that the purpose of shared parental leave was different from that of adoption leave and that the tribunal had not erred in distinguishing between the two. Those differences were held to be both material and significant.'

I'll leave you with the apt lyrics of The Boss, Mr Springsteen, 'You can't start a fire without a spark.'

Baz, Lau, Eliza and George.

THE END.

Unfortunately, the end of the road came for us undeniably so when a potential appeal would cost over ten grand and if we lost, we could be liable to pay the Respondent's fees too. Crowdfunding five grand was a mission. The thought of crowdfunding an additional twenty plus grand was a petrifying thought.

26
Conclusion
Aftermath – Lessons Learned

If I had a pound for everyone who's told me over my lifetime how valuable their principles are to them, I could have filled our crowdfunding pot ten times over! The kinds of folks who sit in the trenches with you, share your cigarettes, and enjoy the camaraderie of the potential battle over the brow. Until it's time to raise your head above the parapet. As you perch tentatively on the brow of the trench, look left, then right, and the comrades looking at you square in the eyes on either flank will be the genuine articles who are willing to put their money where their mouth is. Realistically, there won't be many.

Why the reluctance? And who is to blame? Concerning 'proportionality of blame' the onus is on the Local Authority to be accountable to zero tolerance on any discrimination against employees. However, the government are also accountable as a result of failing to state unequivocally that employers must offer enhanced pay to parents accessing the Shared Parental Leave policy. The Local Authority have pushed integrity aside for the sake of their purse. A short-sighted stance but a business stance.

Whenever there is the existence of a divide and conquering mentality, an 'Us versus Them', the war is already null and void. All the battles between both sides will only serve to perpetuate the division and will ultimately stifle any lasting progressive change. Lots of loud talk and yet nothing is actually said. It all appears to come down to brand value over moral value.

If I had swallowed Morpheus's 'ignorance is bliss' pill, I would not have been signed off with work-related stress and anxiety. I would have focused my energy on positive thoughts, feelings, and actions, and been a more effective family member. However, as I took the blue social justice pill, I learned that attempts at challenging The Man come at a very high personal cost.

Covid has very few positives. That's a given. One of which is that it has shone a blinding light on the inadequacy of UK parental rights, attitudes, policies and provisions. Which makes our challenge all the timelier and more important? For too long politicians have worn extra thick bureaucratic wraparound sunglasses to help ignore the blinding light. It's time to bin the shades, the stereotypical blinkers, and fully embrace the needs and rights of UK parents to ensure we narrow not only the gender pay gap, but the gender care gap too. It's time to cut the bullshit, turn a page and shift our archaic cultural norms as we rebuild our post Covid economy, by establishing fairness and equality for all parents within the workforce.

According to the Trades Union Congress, TUC research found that the level of paid maternity leave for employed women in the UK (six weeks at 90% of average weekly earnings, 33 weeks at £151.20) is one of the lowest in Europe, ranking twenty-two out of twenty-four among European countries. Additionally, one in four fathers don't qualify for two weeks of paternity leave, paid at £151.20. Mothers who are on zero-hour contracts, self-employed or unemployed receive maternity allowance of £151.20 per week for thirty-nine weeks, and there is no equivalent for their partners.

According to The Guardian article by Alexandra Topping in early February 2021, where I read the previous statistics, 'Campaigners including the TUC, the Fawcett Society, Working Families, the Fatherhood Institute and Maternity Action have called for non-transferable parental leave for fathers, a policy that has been taken up about 90% of the time in Sweden and Iceland.'

It's not as though I've been a sly Trojan Horse awaiting my window of opportunity to strike. It's more like I have been an innocent Frankenstein's Monster. The Authority being Dr Frankenstein. They have created me by grinding me down with their relentless ineptitude.

The Supreme Court in deciding against the aforementioned Ali case has made mums the damsels in distress and shredded any architectural bridge-building blueprints for the bridges across to the mythical land of Gender Equality.

It is not the end of the world that the UK bureaucratic albatross around the neck of parental stereotypes exists for us today. Because if we have helped just a smidge in putting the wheels in motion, we can only hope that by 2050 when my daughter Eliza will be thirty-two and son George will be thirty (Gods and Oprah Winfrey willing) their norm will be one of progressiveness, empathy, and empowerment for everyone. Regardless of their sex, where they can be the owner of their destiny minus the 2020 deadwood of bygone anchors of nonsensical policies.

If I was to offer any advice, it would be to know your

grievance inside out and befriend the policies that are involved, e.g. sex discrimination. On your own you are an ant to be squashed beneath the treads of the corporate shoe. If you use your voice wisely and stand by the courage of convictions, others will follow. Gender discrimination is entrenched within the very DNA of our culture's bureaucratic ethos, so be prepared to accept that you may lose the policy battle, but at least you will always have the moral win.

Beware the anxiety gremlins. Mine mostly enjoyed manifesting itself in a threefold pronged attack. In a labyrinth of hyper-vigilance, early hour rumination, and tension. My jaw took the brunt and when it wasn't tighter than a welder's vice, I contemplated wearing a mouth guard à la Tarantino's character, Richie, from *Dusk till dawn*. 'Richie, put your bit in.'

I noticed it after particularly restless nights when my hand would involuntarily be gripped tightly in my sleep. My palms down to elbows would both feel like I'd been on a Steinway piano removal team and I was the shortest team member.

On particularly bad days I would notice the rigidity of the tension when walking our dog, Dexter. My dog lead carrying hand would appear fine and the opposing hand wouldn't sit relaxed like an anchor at the depths of my pocket. They would rise like a blimp to the uppermost roof of my pocket. It would come to my attention when my coat would be risen enough until the cold evening air would hit my bare skin on my core, above my hips.

Often, I would do a body check-in to gauge how I was fairing. I would ground my feet and work my way slowly up to my scalp. Consciously raising my awareness of each part. On particularly bad days I would notice that my toes would be pointing northward in a rigid rigour-mortis style. My feet resembled Aladdin's slippers. Look after yourself if you make yourself vulnerable. It's not a hobby, so prepare to have your very being tested.

The family unit is the undeniable cornerstone of introducing and sustaining values. The Big Bang of the moral compass if you will. The Great Covid-19 forced experiment implemented a polar shift in the family dynamic. Parental units have had an unprecedented override with a new appreciation for an equal partnership, where old stocks were rendered invalid and a whole new portfolio of potential investments was added to a brand-new spreadsheet. Covid-19 conceived the need to overhaul life as we knew it. None more so than that of the family dynamic. Covid-19 gave birth to an unprecedented and uber-restricted zeitgeist. With families being thrust together within four walls, we scrutinised every aspect of home life, work life, and most importantly, family life. The comfortable notion (for some) of stereotypical gender roles were disbanded in order to reinforce a 'Make-Do' teamwork philosophy. A sink or swim forced dynamic. Never before has the rule book been so impractical. Never before has there been an opportunity for a wholesale change in our attitudes and expectations for life. Wide-scale societal norms were now irrelevant and replaced by a drastically down-sized microcosm of a norm. A norm where people who hadn't exercised in fifteen years took up jogging, a new world where DIY and gardening became king (if you were fortunate enough to have any space to do so that is) and most aptly, a miniature version of a community where the safety, nurture, education, and love for family members was imperative. Every single parent of every single adopted identity became the teacher, the nurturer, the protector, and the role models. Gender bias took a holiday while our human side had the opening to emerge, regardless of the boxes society had previously pigeon-holed us into. The nine to five, five-day week working model was decimated and a new flexible approach had to be implemented to manage the new work/life balance status quo. Businesses survived by diversifying, evolving and playing off the cuff.

Covid-19 became the catalyst for an awakening to the outdated expectations of the traditional dynamic within dual earning families and families in general. The cognitive dissonance previously present as to how parenting was and was always expected to be present within the traditional sense generally unravelled.

Here's to the dawn of parental equality in the United Kingdom. Cheers.

THE END